W9-CJQ-437

History of the
Ancient & Medieval World

Volume 1

Origins of
Humanity

Marshall Cavendish
New York Toronto Sydney

Published in 1996 by
Marshall Cavendish Corporation
99 White Plains Road
Tarrytown, NY 10591-9001
U.S.A.

Editor: Henk Dijkstra
Executive Editor: Paulien Retèl
Revision Editor: Henk Singor
Art Director: Henk Oostenrijk, Studio 87, Utrecht, The Netherlands
Index Editors: Schuurmans & Jonkers, Leiden, The Netherlands
Preface: Laura Tedesco, M.A., Department of Anthropology,
New York University, New York

The History of the Ancient and Medieval World is a completely revised and
updated edition of *The Adventure of Mankind.*
© 1996 by HD Communication Consultants BV, Hilversum, The Netherlands
This edition © 1996 by Marshall Cavendish Corporation, Tarrytown, New York, and
HD Communication Consultants BV, Hilversum, The Netherlands.

Library of Congress Cataloging-in-Publication Data

History of the ancient and medieval world / edited by Henk Dijkstra.
p. cm.
Completely rev. and updated ed. of : The Adventure of mankind (second edition 1996).
Contents:—v.1. Origins of Humanity.
ISBN 0-7614-0352-3 (v.1).—ISBN 0-7614-0351-5 (lib.bdg.:set)
1. History, Ancient—Juvenile literature. 2. Middle Ages—History—Juvenile literature. I. Dijkstra, Henk. II. Title: Adventure of mankind
D117.H57 1996
930—dc20/95-35715

Publisher's Note

The mysteries, intrigues, tragedies, and dramas of our distant and near-distant past come vividly alive in this *History of the Ancient and Medieval World*, one of the most comprehensive, culturally balanced treatments of Western and non-Western history currently available. In a major international effort, a team of noted historians, scholars, and educators from around the world have produced this unique, broad-based thoroughly up-to-date history. Though researched by multicultural academics of the highest level and carefully edited by experts in every era and field from American universities, the *History of the Ancient and Medieval World* is written in an easy, accessible style that appeals to both students and adult readers.

The compact, fluid text is enriched with 2,200 vibrant full-color illustrations and photographs with clarifying captions, enabling the reader to envision each era and event. Each chapter's illustrations consist of original visual documentation, including timeless details of paintings, miniatures, and monuments. Maps, both ancient and modern, are plentiful. An abundance of boxed text highlights aid in guiding the reader through centuries of our planet's history, from the formation of life on earth to the brink of the Renaissance.

The set's eleven individual 144-page volumes, chronological by era, ensure its availability to many simultaneous readers. Each of the encyclopedia's volumes contains a glossary of terms relating to the ancient and medieval worlds, including persons, places, and references often difficult to find in dictionaries and other sources. Each volume includes a time line with corresponding sections on political history, cultural history, and events happening at the same time in other parts of the world. Also included are a bibliography, a list of suggestions for further reading currently in print, and an A-Z index.

The encyclopedia's practical value is greatly enhanced by volume 12, the index volume. Chronicles list important ancient and medieval monarchs, rulers, and pharaohs. There is also a complete time line, glossary, and bibliography. Along with the comprehensive A-Z index, thematic indexes ease the reader's way to major geographical locations: Europe, the Middle East, South America, Africa, and the Far East. They also refer the reader to desired topics: government and politics, arts and culture, trade and economy, religion, wars and battles, and the customs of everyday life.

From the celestial bodies of prehistory to the preserved bodies of ancient Egypt, from ancient Africa to Rome's bread and circuses, from the Jewish resistance to the Children's Crusade, the *History of the Ancient and Medieval World* is a brilliant new light from the past that brings today's turbulent world into sharper focus.

Contents of Encyclopedia

Origins of Humanity

Paintings in the caves of Lascaux

CONTENTS

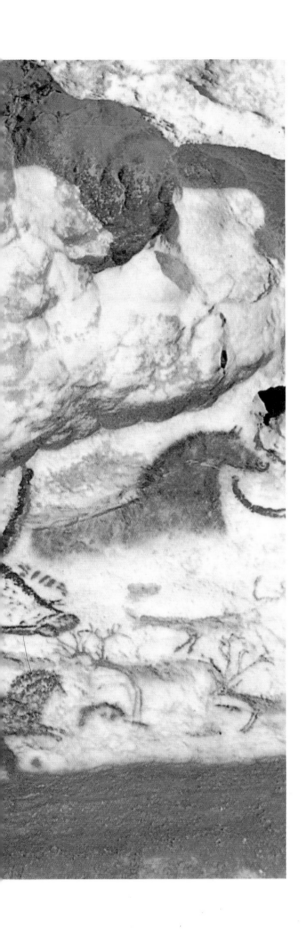

Preface

Volume 1 of *The History of the Ancient and Medieval World* has before it an ambitious task. That is the introduction of the concepts surrounding the creation of Earth and the development of human life and culture up to the historic age. The text begins with an introduction into the theories of the development of the universe, Earth, and earliest life-forms. This sets the geological and biological context for discussion of the evolution of human life and culture.

Sections devoted to the explanation of the basic tenets of evolutionary theory and the archaeological evidence that accounts for the evolution of *Homo sapiens sapiens* are necessary components in this volume. They are an essential background for the presentation of the complex chronicle of human cultural evolution. A practical setting is formed through discussions of the eras of the earliest *Australopithecine* and *Homo* species. The hallmarks of human innovation and culture known from the archaeological record associated with *Homo erectus,* Archaic *Homo sapiens* (Neandertals), and Anatomically Modern Humans (AMH), including the first toolmaking, cave painting, and symbolic representation, are all vital and fascinating elements of this narrative.

The text highlights the inventions of cultures across the globe from the Neolithic period to the end of the Iron Age. The domestication of plants and animals, the invention of writing and metallurgy, and the formation of cities are milestones in the course of increasing human modernization.

Finally, this volume includes detailed sections explaining the expansion of cultures through Europe and the occupation of that land which begins to take the shape of a territory rich in ethnic and cultural diversity. All of the components of this first volume are vital elements to the narrative of worldwide human cultural development that continues today.

Laura Tedesco, M.A.,
Department of Anthropology,
New York University, New York

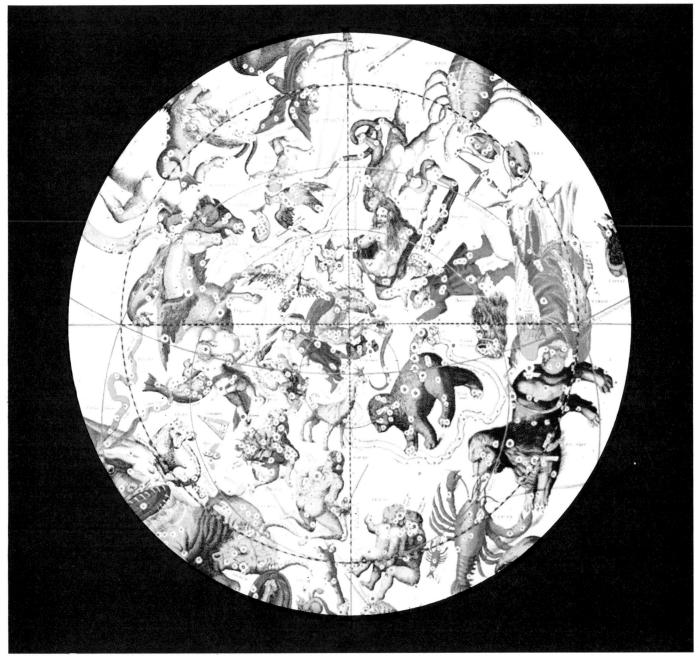

The star-spangled sky with the astrological figures and names that were used in astronomy to denote constellations. Colored copper engraving, seventeenth century

The Universe

The Development of Astronomy

Astronomy is perhaps the oldest branch of science. Drawings of constellations scratched on sea urchins and stones at the end of the Paleolithic era (more than 10,000 years ago) have been found in France and Russia. The ancient Egyptians, Assyrians, Chinese, and Greeks were all acute observers of the world above them.

The Greeks saw the world in the light of their perceptions of the Sun, the Moon, and the stars. They interpreted the world through their mythology until about the fifth century BC. As they observed the night sky, they saw certain bodies traveling in established orbits rather than holding to fixed positions. Unaware that these are not stars, but are only reflecting the light of the Sun, they named them planetes, or wandering stars.

About 530 BC, Pythagoras, a Greek philosopher and mathematician, settled in Crotona, a Greek colony in southern Italy. During his extensive travels he had noticed that his walking stick cast an increasingly shorter shadow as the noon hour approached when he was in countries nearer the equator. From this he deduced that Earth was round. He and his followers were the first to view Earth as a sphere revolving with other planets around a central fire. About 450 BC, one of his followers, Philolaus, postulated that

Earth, the Sun, the Moon, and the planets all revolved around a central fire that could not be seen because a counterearth hid it. Philolaus contended that the revolution of Earth around that fire every twenty-four hours explained the movements of the Sun and the stars. Eudoxus of Cnidus offered another theory in 370 BC. He thought Earth was inside a giant sphere that had the stars attached to its inner surface. It rotated daily around Earth and also held other smaller spheres, which he believed explained planetary motion.

Another Greek, Aristarchus of Samos, believed that Earth turned on its axis once every twenty-four hours. Like Pythagoras, he felt that Earth and the other planets revolved around a fire but that the fire was the Sun. Most of the ancient Greeks remained unconvinced, holding to a belief in geocentrism, or an Earth-centered universe around which the other celestial bodies spun. Appolonius, in the second century BC, developed a complicated theory to explain the planetary orbits that he observed. He suspected that even as the planets moved in their orbit around Earth, they traveled another circular path, the epicycle. This is a small circle centered on the rim of a larger circle, somewhat like a key ring spinning on a wire bracelet.

In the second century AD, the Greek astronomers Ptolemy and Hipparchus charted the positions of about a thousand stars they observed revolving in fixed patterns around the North Pole. These were the constellations of the zodiac, stars seen some eight degrees each side of the ecliptic

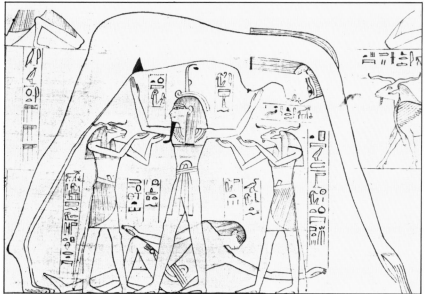

In this Egyptian representation of the cosmos the sky goddess, Nut, arches over the recumbent earth god, Geb.
The air god, Shu, supports the firmament.
Papyrus vignette, c.1000 BC

The telescopes of the European Southern Observatory on La Silla Mountain in Chile

(the apparent path of the Sun among the stars). The zodiac included the orbits of the Sun, the Moon, and the five planets they recognized (Mercury, Venus, Mars, Jupiter, and Saturn). They divided this celestial belt into twelve sections, or signs of the zodiac, apparently adopting signs already in use in Mesopotamia. In his work *Almagest,* Ptolemy explained the motion of these bodies by saying each moved in its own orbit around Earth and around a second circle, an epicycle.

Not until the sixteenth century AD was there a challenge put to the Aristotelian and Ptolemaic assumption that planets circle a fixed Earth. The Polish astronomer Nicolaus Copernicus postulated a heliocentric (sun-centered) solar system (from helios, the Greek word for sun). He saw Earth as rotating daily on its axis and revolving annually around the Sun. The planets, he contended, circled the Sun. (Their orbits later proved to be elliptical and the speed at which they revolve inconsistent.)

Copernicus's views were not published until after his death to avoid conflict with the powerful Roman Catholic Church, which regarded them as heretical. In 1616 his books were subjected to censorship. He had few followers, but they included the German astronomer Johannes Kepler, who deduced three laws that first described the motions of each of the known planets.

The laws of Kepler state that 1) the orbit of a planet around the Sun is an ellipse, 2) the planet moves fastest when closest to the Sun, slowest when distant, and 3) the square of the time for one revolution about the Sun equals the cube of its mean distance from the Sun's center. Kepler's second law expresses the conservation of angular momentum. Kepler's third law, in generalized form, can be stated as follows: The square of the period (in years) times the total mass (measured in solar masses) equals the cube of the mean distance (in astronomical units). This last law permits the masses of the planets to be calculated by measuring the size and period of satellite orbits.

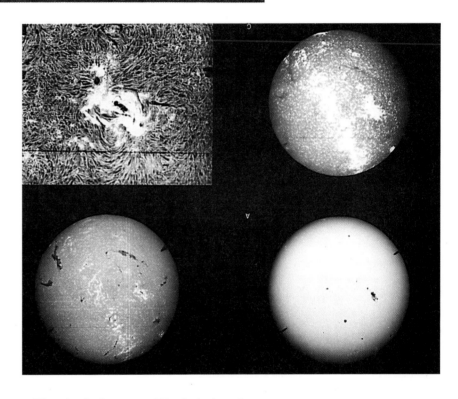

The physical causes of Kepler's three laws were later explained by the English mathematician and physicist Sir Isaac Newton, one of the greatest scientists of all time and another Copernican. (Newton's work had convinced the influential intelligentsia of England, France, Denmark, and the Netherlands by the end of the seventeenth century. The rest of Europe remained hostile to Copernicus for another hundred years.)

The Sun, photographed in four different ways: white, red, violet, and roentgen light

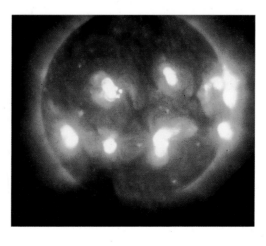

The Sun observed through X rays, September 5, 1973

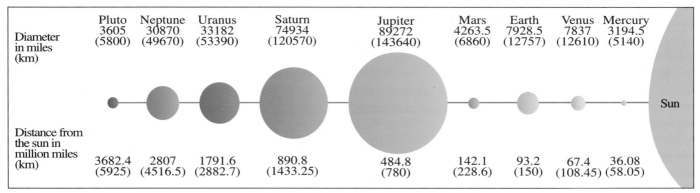

	Pluto	Neptune	Uranus	Saturn	Jupiter	Mars	Earth	Venus	Mercury
Diameter in miles (km)	3605 (5800)	30870 (49670)	33182 (53390)	74934 (120570)	89272 (143640)	4263.5 (6860)	7928.5 (12757)	7837 (12610)	3194.5 (5140)
Distance from the sun in million miles (km)	3682.4 (5925)	2807 (4516.5)	1791.6 (2882.7)	890.8 (1433.25)	484.8 (780)	142.1 (228.6)	93.2 (150)	67.4 (108.45)	36.08 (58.05)

Scale model of the Sun and the planets of our solar system. The temperature on the planets closest to the Sun is extremely high; the farther the distance from the Sun, the colder it gets. Earth is the only planet with moderate temperatures, which are suitable to sustain animal and plant life.

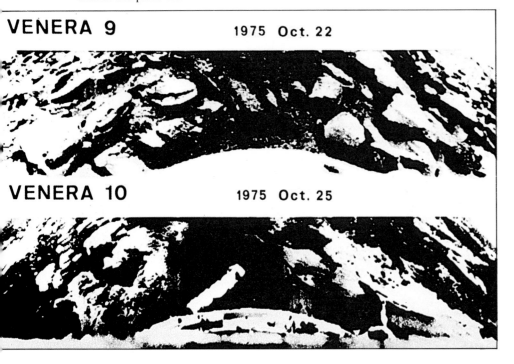

VENERA 9 — 1975 Oct. 22

VENERA 10 — 1975 Oct. 25

The surface of Venus, as photographed by the *Venera* spacecraft in 1975. The extreme heat and high pressure of its atmosphere caused the cameras on board to fail after only twenty minutes.

The Italian physicist and astronomer Galileo Galilei was the first person to build an optical telescope, adapting the concept from the newly invented Dutch spyglass. With it he saw mountains and craters on the Moon and discovered sunspots and four moons around Jupiter. He also learned that the Milky Way was made of stars. His findings, published in 1610 in the *Starry Messenger,* were a major contribution to astronomy. His observations of the phases of Venus reinforced his belief in Copernican theory, which supported his own theory on the tides, described in 1624 in his *Dialogue on the Tides.* Galileo had been told to stop defending the concept that Earth moves. After he wrote an open letter to the Church contending that the Bible was irrelevant to science, he was tried, convicted, and ultimately sentenced to permanent house arrest in 1633. He continued to work, postulating the laws of falling bodies and the motions of projectiles. He made physics a science of precise measurement rather than philosophy and logic. Galileo's work represents a triumph of freedom of thought against authority.

Newton invented calculus in 1666. In the field of optics, he explained color as rays of varied length. As proof he passed a beam of sunlight through a prism to divide it into its separate colors. He is most famous for his three laws of motion, which he applied to Kepler's laws of orbital motion, deriving the law of universal gravitation: that all bodies in space and on Earth are affected by gravity. He explained the theory in his book *Philosophiae Naturalis Principia Mathematica* in 1687, a turning point in science.

If you look at the sky at night, you will see that not all stars are equally bright and that stars have different colors. Some are reddish, others bluish white in color. This color difference has to do with their surface tempera-

The surface of Mars as photographed during the Mars explorations by *Mariner* in 1965

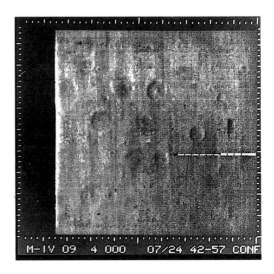

ture, just as white-hot iron is hotter than red-hot iron. The study of both the brightness (photometry) and the color (spectroscopy) of starlight is an integral part of modern astronomy. The telescope is essential to each.

Galileo's telescope had a lens opening of just over an inch (2.54 centimeters). Those made by the Herschels, Sir William and his sister Caroline, German-born British astronomers, were far larger and constantly improved. Sir William discovered the planet Uranus in 1781. A new telescope he built at Slough, a town west of London, had a 48-inch (1.2-meter) mirror and a focal length of 40 feet (12 meters); with it he discovered two satellites of Uranus and the sixth and seventh satellites of Saturn. (Today's largest optic telescopes have mirror diameters of about 26 feet or 8 meters.) Galileo studied the motion of planets and double stars (two stars so close together they appear as one), cataloging over 800 double stars. He observed some 2,500 nebulae (the Latin plural for clouds) and was the first to consider them to be composed of stars.

Before the Herschels, the term nebula was used for any hazy objects visible in the night sky, including star clusters or galaxies. In astronomy today, nebula refers to a localized conglomerate of interstellar gas, dust, or both.

Considered by many as the founder of sidereal (star) astronomy, William Herschel

was elected to the Royal Society in 1781 and knighted in 1816. His sister discovered three nebulae and eight comets. Comets are celestial bodies of small mass that revolve around the Sun. Each is composed of a relatively dense mass of dust, gas, or a mixture of each. (Some fifty comets appear at regular intervals. The best documented is Halley's comet.)

Caroline Herschel cataloged the findings of her brother and the first Royal

Io, one of Jupiter's moons, as seen by *Voyager I*. Active volcanos have been discovered there.

Jupiter, photographed from a distance of 33.5 million miles (54 million kilometers) by *Voyager I*. Jupiter is one of the largest planets of our solar system.

11

Astronomer of England, John Flamsteed, in *Historia Coelestis Britannica*. Completed in 1725, it listed over 3,000 stars and corrected contemporary errors in astronomical tables. Newton was able to verify his theory of gravity using Flamsteed's lunar observations.

At the beginning of the nineteenth century, the invention of spectroscopy and photography had a great impact on astronomy. Spectroscopy, or spectral analysis, is based on the fact that every chemical element possesses its own characteristic spectrum. Under certain conditions, each element emits light in characteristic colors that constitute a

Voyager II's 1980 photograph of the rings of Saturn, which consist of the remains of a former moon.

color fingerprint. Color itself has specific wavelengths. For example, red light has a longer wavelength than blue light. The infrared rays invisible to the human eye have a longer wavelength than red light. Starlight shining through a narrow opening and then through a prism is sorted into wavelengths of color. This rainbow of colored lines, arranged by order of wavelength, is called a spectrum. The individual bands of color are called spectral lines, identifiable by wavelength.

Under certain conditions, an element also absorbs light in characteristic wavelengths. The Bavarian optician and physicist Joseph von Fraunhofer (1787–1826) first observed and mapped the dark lines visible in the spectrum of the Sun. Apparently, light is absorbed in these dark zones. By comparing the lines (later to be given his name) with absorption spectra (the Latin plural for spectrum) already recognized in the laboratory,

the elements that make up the Sun could be determined and the composition and surface temperature of stars ascertained.

Fraunhofer developed new techniques for the making of optical glass, grinding and polishing lenses, and building telescopes. He was the inventor of several scientific instruments. His studies in light led to the invention of the spectroscope in 1959 by the Germans Gustav Robert Kirchhoff and Robert Wilhelm Bunsen. This laid the groundwork for spectral analysis, the determination of each element's unique spectrum (used for chemical analysis). A year later, the two used their technique to discover the elements cesium and rubidium.

Since the light sent by celestial spectra is usually quite weak, precise analysis required photography. Spectral analysis proved to yield an unexpected wealth of information. It was possible, for example, to determine whether or not the stars studied were approaching Earth or moving away from it, whether they possessed magnetic fields, and whether or not they were accompanied by other stars (then termed double stars). These could be separately measured for mass and brightness using the techniques of photometry.

Photometry measures the brightness or the luminous intensity of a light source with the use of photometers. Photometers approximate the human eye, which is much more sensitive, receiving different degrees of stimulation depending on the wavelength of the light waves observed. Colored filters are used to make photometers respond more like the human eye. Light is measured in units of candle power. Instruments called radiometers are used to measure radiant energy and are equally sensitive to all wavelengths.

Astronomy today combines the insights of physics with the observations made by telescope and satellite. It also uses far more than the information from the visible part of the electromagnetic spectrum, deploying radio, infrared, ultraviolet, Roentgen, and gamma-ray sensitive "eyes" into space.

A picture of Earth taken with a camera onboard *Apollo VIII*, the first manned spacecraft to orbit the Moon, December, 1968

The Universe Today

A Picture of Space

The center of our solar system is the Sun, which is a star. Like other stars, it is made up of hot gases (hydrogen and helium) held together by gravity. The Sun emits electromagnetic radiation because of the nuclear reactions going on inside its core. Light, essential to life as we know it on Earth, is part of that radiation. Light comes from the visible surface of the Sun, called the photosphere, with a temperature of about 10,000 °F (5,540°C). Areas of cooler temperature on that surface appear as sunspots. The surface is not quiet; bursts of gases and energy called prominences and solar flares continually erupt, sending out a stream of particles (mostly protons) called the solar wind. Solar energy is radiated out into space from the surface at 3.8 X (1 X 10^{26}). (1 X 10^{26} means

1 with 26 zeros.) This, in turn, is responsible for the aurora borealis, the northern lights. The Sun has a thick atmosphere, the corona, consisting of hot gases only seen during a total solar eclipse.

The distance from Earth to the Sun is 93 million miles (150 million kilometers). Astronomic distance is expressed in terms of the speed of light, about 186,000 miles (300,000 kilometers) per second. A light-year is the distance light travels in one year. Since there are about 30 million seconds in a year, a light-year is a distance of about 5,900 billion miles (9,495 billion kilometers), roughly 6 trillion miles (9.5 trillion kilometers). Sunlight takes eight minutes to cover this distance, so we see the Sun the way it

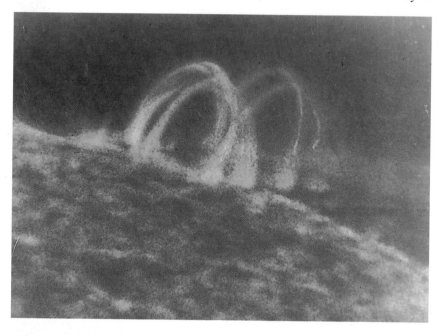

Gas explosion
on the surface of
the Sun

looked eight minutes ago. The distance equals eight light-minutes.

The Sun is only an average-sized star compared to hundreds of billions of others in our galaxy alone, the band of stars called the Milky Way. About 4,000 of them can be seen from each hemisphere with the unaided eye. Our solar system revolves around the center of the Milky Way, 30,000 light-years away.

The Milky Way is only one of several hundred million galaxies discernible through modern telescopes. Galaxies occur in clusters, kept together by mutual gravity.

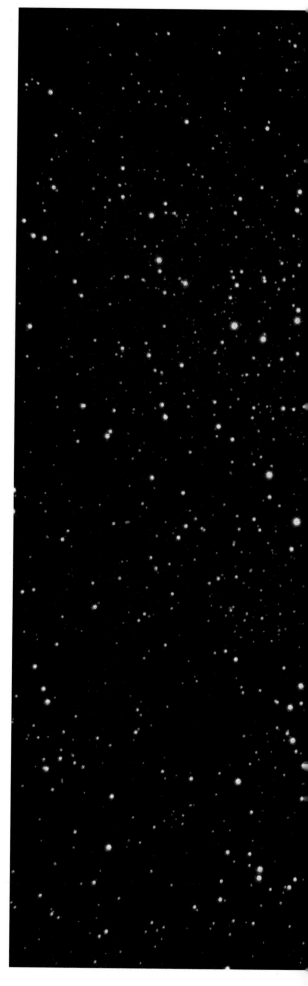

Wide-angle
view of the center of
the Milky Way

14

Clusters are grouped into superclusters. Some galaxies are irregular in shape. The two small irregular galaxies neighboring the Milky Way were named the large and small Magellanic Clouds before separate stars could be identified in them. Many galaxies, like the galaxy called M87, are spherical. From an outside point, our galaxy looks like a flattened disk with a spiral structure. Its diameter is approximately 100,000 light-years. Our solar system is a mere speck in this great spinning spiral. There are many other spiral galaxies in space. One is the Andromeda galaxy, 2,000,000 light-years away and twenty times the size of ours.

The American astronomer Edwin Hubble identified and measured individual pulsating stars in Andromeda and other nebulae in 1924. Comparing their periods of pulsation and brightness with nearer stars, Hubble proved that these nebulae are outside our galaxy.

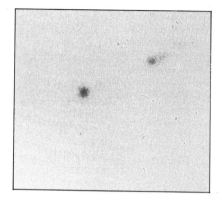
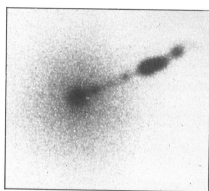
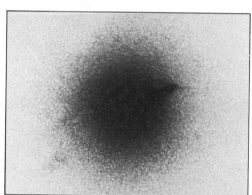

Three views of the giant elliptical system M87, with its active center.

Hubble's Law

According to Albert Einstein, space and time are inseparable. The farther we see into space, the further back in time we look. This has consequences for determining the age of the universe. Distant constellations, called quasars, for quasi–stellar object, show a different age than the closer stars they look like. The light that reaches us now from constellations ten billion light-years away was emitted ten billion years ago, establishing them as far younger than the closer stars. That light indicated that other galaxies were moving away from ours at several hundred miles per second.

The way these other galaxies appeared to move away from the Milky Way seemed to prove the Milky Way was the center of the universe. The red shift of constellations,

The Andromeda nebula

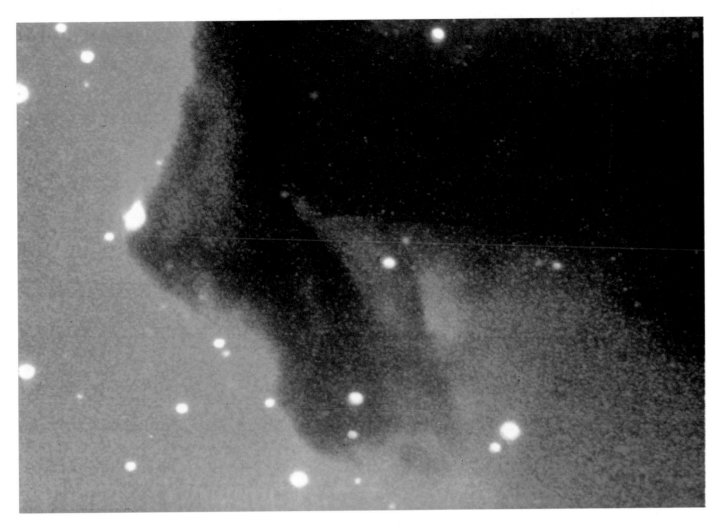

an effect first observed by American astronomer Vesto M. Slipher in 1912, seemed to explain that. The spectrum of a constellation is at the red end of the visual spectrum. Each element emits a unique collection of colors, or spectral lines. The hydrogen spectral lines from quasars and other galaxies have the same "fingerprint" as hydrogen lines here on Earth, but shifted in color toward the red. This was clarified by Hubble in 1929. He observed that the greater the distance of the galaxy, the faster its recession velocity. The galaxies moved away from Earth at a speed proportional to the amount of red shift, with a recession velocity proportional to their distance. This is called the law of the red shift, or Hubble's Law.

The universe expands uniformly like a balloon. Imagine the Milky Way as a balloon with evenly spaced dots painted on it, each one a galaxy. As the balloon is inflated, all the points (galaxies) move farther apart. We see all the galaxies moving away from our viewpoint in like manner.

The Birth and Death of Stars
In the thin gas of the Milky Way that is called interstellar matter, condensation occurs. If the increasingly dense cloud of gas becomes heavy enough, it collapses under the effect of its own gravity and contracts into a sphere. As a result, the gas is heated, increasing its pressure. If the temperature in the center of this ball of gas reaches approximately 27 million °F (15 million °C), then nuclear fusion–the combining of two atoms of a simple element to make another element –commences and a new star is born. In the nuclear fusion of hydrogen that goes on in the Sun, the element helium is created and energy is produced.

Stars can be formed with masses ranging from 0.08 to about 120 solar masses. The life history of stars depends on their mass. The Sun has one solar mass; stars like the Sun will live for about 10 billion years, spending their fuel slowly, while the more massive stars will live only millions of years.

As an average-sized star (0.5 to 3 solar masses) reaches the end of its life, it grows into a giant red star. (The Sun is expected to swallow Mercury and Venus as it grows. Its size will eventually make life on Earth impossible.) In the later stages of its life, such a star may fluctuate in size, pulsating from small to large. Its core gets so hot that the radiation it emits ejects its outer layers

Horse's Head nebula; a cloud of dark gas and dust

17

The Pleiaden
constellation

into space, revealing a small hot core called a white dwarf star. This white dwarf slowly cools over billions of years (unless it is part of a binary star system). Most of the stars in our universe are binaries. When a white dwarf and a red giant orbit one another, the white dwarf will suck mass from the red giant until the surface of the white dwarf explodes. This type of explosion is called a nova (new star) and is coupled with a sudden strong increase in light intensity. The same pair can repeat this "performance" many times, resulting in many brilliant novas. If two white dwarfs orbit one another and then spiral in, collide, and explode, the result is a much brighter supernova, Type I.

A heavy star (10 to 100 solar masses) also ends its life with an enormous explosion, which throws its outer layers into space, creating a supernova, Type II. In this case, the star's core continues the fusion process until iron is made in the core. Iron will not fuse. The star's gravitational forces cause a collapse of Earth-sized iron core in 0.1 seconds. This collapse is quickly followed by a stupendous rise in core temperature, an outpouring of mass, and a huge burst of radiation. With this explosion, most of the star's mass is ejected into space. (Much later,

other stars will form from the mass released in the explosion. All of the heavy elements on Earth were generated during such supernova explosions.)

The iron core collapses and changes into neutrons that form a neutron star or, in extremely heavy stars, a black hole. (The nucleus of an atom, orbited by negatively charged electrons, normally comprises neutrons and positively charged protons.) A neutron star is extremely small (about 20 miles or 32 kilometers in diameter) and heavy. (One teaspoonful of a neutron star would weigh 100 million tons or 1 trillion kilograms.) It rotates unbelievably fast and possesses strong magnetic fields. Particles can escape this field only at the poles of the stars. As they rotate, neutron stars throw off a stream of particles perceived on Earth as periodic pulsations, much like light cast from a lighthouse. Hence they are called pulsars. Pulsing times as short as 0.03 seconds have been recorded. Imagine an object 20 miles (32 kilometers) in diameter (like New York City) rotating thirty times per second!

The density of a black hole is assumed to be considerably greater than that of a neutron star. Its gravity is so great that all matter and radiation moving into what is termed the Schwarzschild radius will be swallowed up. It was Albert Einstein who first reported the existence of black holes, which can be observed only indirectly by the intense X rays and gamma-rays emitted by matter falling into them. The evolution of X-ray and gamma-ray astronomy has already made possible the detection of ten probable locations of black holes. It is believed that a black hole millions of solar masses in size may be at the center of our galaxy.

Cosmology

The field of cosmology studies the past and future of our universe. Einstein's General Theory of Relativity introduced complex gravitational equations in which the key parameter is the density of matter in the universe. If the universe started with the explosion of a "primeval atom" (see Big Bang Theory this page), then the universe will expand forever, but only if the average matter density is below the critical value of 18×10^{-28} pounds/-in^3 (5×10^{-30} grams/cc). However, if the average density is above this value, then the gravitational attraction among the galaxies will force the expansion to stop and reverse. The ensuing contraction will collapse the universe back to a primeval atom, which may explode again. This cycle will repeat over and over, in an oscillating universe model.

In 1948 British astronomers, philosophically opposed to the concept of a changing universe, proposed a "steady state" model of the universe. To counter the idea of the expansion of the universe, with its decreasing density of space, they introduced the notion of the continuous creation of matter to balance the expansion. This constant creation of matter would forever maintain the present appearance of the universe.

This model of the universe, called the steady state theory, is no longer accepted, mainly because when we look back in time to the early universe, we see many violently active galaxies called quasars (for quasi-stellar radio sources) that are not seen in the more recent past. It is thought that these radio sources several billion light-years away are early galaxies with massive black holes at their centers. Their tremendous outpouring of energy that we see here on Earth is thought to be a result of a great inpouring of matter.

Other cosmological speculations have included the notion that ours is but one of many millions of universes that are continuously being produced as the effect of a basic instability. Beginning with the early concept of Earth as the center of a very limited universe, the human intellect has pushed the center farther and farther away.

The Age of the Universe

If the rate of expansion of the universe is known, its age can be estimated by deter-

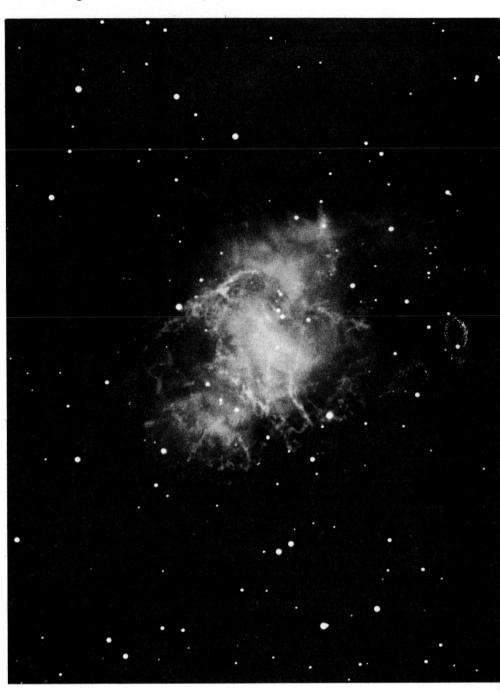

mining the time it took for the universe to reach its present size. Present estimates range between 7 and 15 billion years. However, the age of some stars seems to be older than the estimated age of the universe. This paradox is now being hotly debated.

The Big Bang Theory

The Russian-American physicist George Gamow proposed the most widely accepted theory of the origin of the universe in 1948.

The Crab nebula, located in the constellation Taurus. It is the remnant of the supernova explosion observed by Chinese astronomers in AD 1054 .

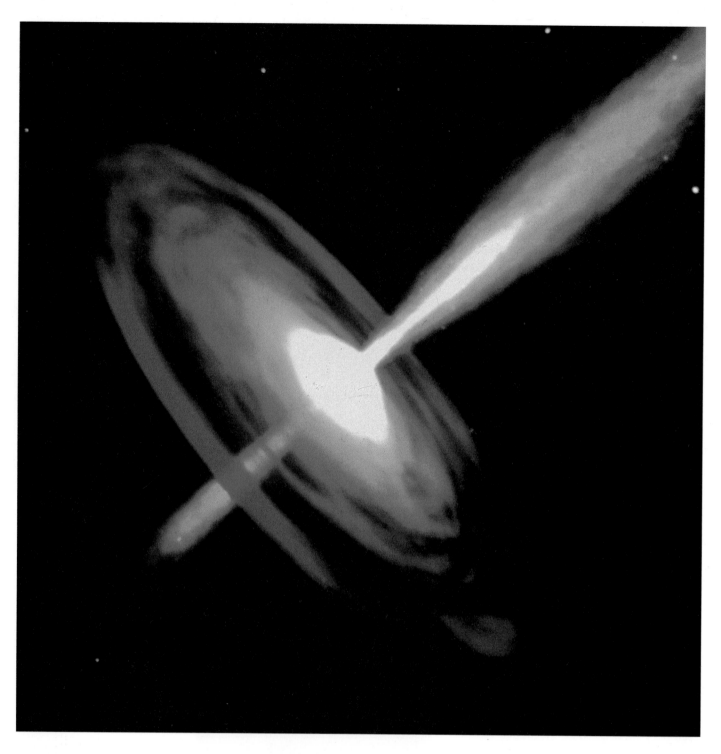

Galactic
black hole and
optical jet

Called the big bang theory, it postulated that the universe was created in the gigantic explosion of a primeval atom. Immediately after the big bang, according to Gamow, subatomic particles influenced by the great temperature and pressure were fused into the elements known today. Further calculation has led to the contention that it was primarily hydrogen and helium that were created. The enormous density of the primeval atom would have caused the universe to expand rapidly. Other elements are thought to have been created later by stars that were themselves the condensed product of cooled hydrogen and helium.

Much current work in theoretical cosmology is centered on developing a better understanding of the processes that must have shaped the big bang. Assuming that the universe is still expanding, residual radiation from the initial explosion would be expected to have cooled by this time to about -454 °F or -270°C. Radio astronomy detected residual radiation of this temperature in 1965, thus confirming the theory in the view of most astronomers.

New Techniques of Observation

The human eye is sensitive to only a relatively small range of wavelengths within the total electromagnetic spectrum; rays with a longer wavelength than red light, or a shorter wavelength than ultraviolet light, cannot be seen by humans. The atmosphere of Earth is not transparent to certain rays. The ozone layer, some 12 to 15 miles (19 to 24 kilometers) above Earth's surface, absorbs most of the Sun's ultraviolet rays. Astronomers would like to detect those rays still invisible to us from space. They have been able to accomplish this in branches of astronomy that developed out of the radio astronomy that originated in 1945. Radio frequencies offer a far greater view of distant objects than that provided by waves in the visible spectrum. Rays that cannot penetrate Earth's atmosphere can be detected by radio telescopes mounted on satellites.

Satellites have been sending images of galaxies and stars down to Earth by processing infrared, ultraviolet, and X-ray sections of the electromagnetic spectrum. The Hubble telescope, in particular, adjusted in space by American astronauts in 1995, has sent down spectacular images from space with far better resolution than obtainable from Earth. Technology is currently being developed that may allow large Earth-based

Ring nebula
in the Aquarius
constellation

The Andromeda galaxy
is the nearest neighbor to
our own Milky Way,
at about 2 million lightyears
from Earth.

21

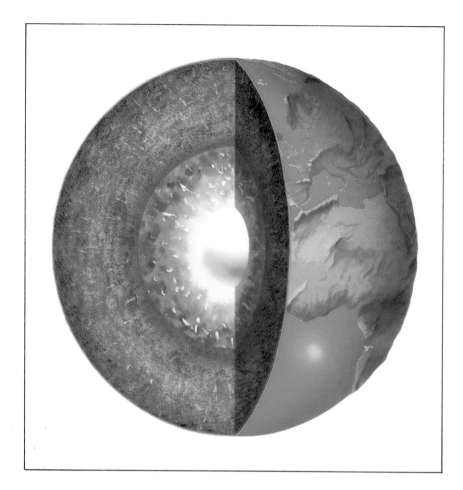

Schematic section of Earth

telescopes to equal or exceed the resolution from the smaller Hubble.

The Solar System

By definition, a solar system is a star and the celestial bodies that orbit around it. Ours comprises the Sun, nine planets and their satellites (whether Pluto is one is being debated), and the smaller bodies (asteroids or meteoroids) that revolve around it. The planets appear to shine because they reflect the Sun's light. They don't really shine like stars. Distances are measured in the astronomical unit (AU), which is the mean distance from Earth to the Sun (93 million miles, or 150 million kilometers). The heliopause, the border between the Earth and the interstellar space, begins at about 100 AU.

It is thought that when the Sun formed, 4.7 billion years ago, there were not yet any planets. The Sun, according to this theory, formed from the dense center of a solar nebula caused by the breakup and gravitational collapse of an interstellar cloud of gas and dust. That such clouds tend to fragment into multiple systems is evident by the large number of binary stars and the many moons of Jupiter and Saturn.

Meteor crater in Arizona. This crater was created by the impact of a meteoric stone. It is 2,640 feet (1,500 meters) in diameter and 650 feet (200 meters) in depth.

According to this theory, the young Sun was very active. A powerful solar wind blew gases and volatile elements out from the inner core. Here the temperature was higher than it was nearer the periphery. This temperature discrepancy created a chemical division of the matter in the disk. The Sun was surrounded by microscopic particles and gas that adhered to each other. Over the next 100 million years, larger objects called planetesimals formed from the particles and gas, creating the predecessors of planets.

Planetesimals near the Sun consisted of stones and oxides of metals, which later formed the inner terrestrial planets Mercury, Venus, Earth, and Mars. Hydrogen, helium, and ice accumulated in the outer parts of the nebula, giving rise to the giant gaseous planets, Jupiter, Saturn, Uranus, and Neptune, as well as tiny, more solid Pluto.

The planets, except for Pluto, rotate in a virtually flat plane around the Sun. Except for Venus and Uranus, the planets orbit in a counterclockwise direction, rotating on their axes in the same direction. Satellites, in general, rotate in the same direction as the planets they orbit, but Jupiter, Saturn, and Neptune each have one or more moons that move clockwise.

Lying between Mars and Jupiter is an asteroid belt, a zone of rocky bodies orbiting the Sun. They range in size from the 620-mile (1,000-kilometer) diameter of the one called Ceres to tiny stones. Pieces of asteroids resulting from collisions are called meteoroids.

The orbits of comets, extending far into outer space, form something of a sphere around the Sun. Comets have a solid nucleus surrounded by a coma (or head) of dust particles and frozen gases about 3 to 6 miles (5 to 10 kilometers) in diameter. When their great swings bring them near the Sun, some of this matter evaporates from the comet's interior, forming the characteristic tail. Some comets, attracted by the gravitational field of Jupiter, have relatively small orbits that bring them regularly into our solar system. Halley's comet returns to our view every seventy-five years; it was last seen in 1986.

The Creation of Earth

Like all planets in our solar system, Earth was created from the collision and fusing of chunks of rock or planetesimals. The larger the early (or proto) planet became, the more difficult it was for the heat created in the collisions to be released. The planet's volume increased faster than its surface area.

Heavy elements like iron sank through the molten matter to the center of the

protoplanet, forming a solid core. Lighter components rose to the surface by definition. Earth became a planet once that core was formed, 4.57 billion years ago. A huge wave of heat ran from the core to Earth's molten surface where the temperature was 3,650 °F (2,000 °C). There was not yet any solid crust.

Meteoroids, small solid bodies from space, whizzed into the atmosphere, incandescent from the resulting friction. Meteorites (meteors reaching the surface of Earth or another planet) frequently hit the

planet. An estimated 4.4 billion years ago a huge meteorite almost the size of Mars crashed into Earth. The catastrophic explosion destroyed the meteorite. Some of its matter entered into orbit around Earth, coalescing (clumping together) into the Moon. (Not every planetary moon has such a dramatic history. Planetesimals can be caught by the field of gravity of a planet and continue to circle it as moons.)

The atmosphere of Earth contained almost no oxygen 4.5 billion years ago. Gases stored in the rocks were released. They were similar in composition to those of present-day volcanic gases: water, nitrogen, and carbon dioxide. Once the atmosphere became

Edward Aldrin of *Apollo XI* is installing instruments for seismographic measuring on the Moon.

23

saturated with water vapor, it rained. Oceans formed and landmasses developed, marked by emerging mountains and water systems.

New Planets

In October 1995 two independent teams of astronomers announced the first discovery of a planet orbiting a star similar to the Sun. If their sightings are valid, it increases the

Earth with the moon in the foreground, taken by the astronauts of *Apollo VIII,* December 1968

chances that our solar system is not unique and that there may be life on other planets.

The new planet, discovered first by Michael Mayor and Didier Queloz of the Geneva Observatory in Switzerland, was confirmed by the Americans Geoffrey Marcy and Paul Butler, working at the Lick Observatory near San Jose, California.

The planet is estimated to be about half the size of Jupiter. It is in rapid orbit (once every four Earth days) around the star Pegasus 51, some forty light-years from Earth. (In comparison, Mercury, the planet in our solar system closest to the Sun, orbits every eighty-eight days.) The temperature of Pegasus 51 is about 1,800 °F (980°C), hot enough to

drive off a gaseous atmosphere unless it were a hydrogen planet the size of Jupiter. Pegasus 51 is some 8 billion years old, compared to our Sun's age of 5 billion years. The star, but not the planet, is visible to the unaided eye in the Northern Hemisphere.

This may be only the first of many such sightings. In October 1995 astronomers from the California Institute of Technology, working at the Palomar Observatory in California, also announced the sighting of another possible planet orbiting the star GL229, some thirty light-years from Earth.

Prior to this, the only other evidence of the existence of planets outside this solar system came from the sightings of Dr. Alexander Wolszczan of Pennsylvania State University in 1992. He discovered two planets, and possibly a moon-sized third one, orbiting a pulsar (dead star). All of these planets are unlikely to support life.

Our Place in the Universe

The Planets

Mercury (3,030 miles or 4,880 kilometers in diameter) has a density approximately equal to that of Earth, a large iron core, and a thin atmosphere of sodium, potassium, helium, hydrogen, and oxygen. Photographs taken by the Mariner 10 space probe in 1974 and again in 1975 show a crater-pocked surface of dark rock. The probe recorded temperatures of 810°F (432°C) on the Sun's side and -290°F (-179°C) on the dark side. Orbiting in a slightly inclined plane (7 degrees) relative to the other planets, Mercury's mean distance from the Sun is about 36 million miles (58 million kilometers). It revolves about the Sun every 88 days, rotating on its axis every 58.7 days.

Venus, brightest object in the sky, has phases like the Moon, and is visible the three hours before sunrise when it is called the morning star and three hours after sunset, as the evening star. A mean distance of 67 million miles (108.58 kilometers) from the Sun,

Venus revolves around the Sun every .62 percent of a year and takes 243 Earth days to rotate on its axis. It has an atmosphere of 97 percent carbon dioxide with traces of water, nitrogen, argon, carbon monoxide, neon, and sulfur dioxide. Because its atmosphere is 31 miles (50 kilometers) deep and ninety times thicker than Earth's, a greenhouse effect results, making Venus the hottest planet, with a surface temperature of about 890°F (478°C). Night-side temperatures reach -27.4°F (-33°C.) Venus has a mass . 82 percent of Earth's. It has been investigated by a number of space vehicles since the first American flyby, Mariner 2, in 1962. (The Soviet Union has sent over a dozen Veñera orbiters since 1967, as well as probes that have reached the planet's surface. In 1978 the United States sent two Pioneer Venus missions. Pioneer Venus 2 sent four probes to the surface, leaving the rest in the upper atmosphere. The orbiter Pioneer Venus 1 continues to pass through and measure the upper atmosphere daily. The American Magellan probe has been transmitting radar images of Venus since 1990. A topographic map of most of the planet has been made, using American and Russian data. It shows the surface to be an extensive plain banded by two massive highland regions.

Mars (.11 percent of Earth's mass) is a mean distance of 141.6 million miles (227.1 million kilometers) from the Sun. The heavy oxidation (or rust) of its surface colors it red and orange. Regions of color change with the Martian seasons, as does the size of the planet's polar caps, which are of solid carbon dioxide, or dry ice. There is evidence that the

On Taal volcano in the Philippines, there are fumaroles in a lake located on top of the large volcanic crater. Volcanoes and earthquakes are the clearest signs of continuous metamorphic activities on Earth.

The crust of Earth is subject to continuous change. In 1963 the new island of Surtsey emerged off the coast of Iceland after a volcanic undersea eruption.

26

planet once had water on its surface, but it is now dry and cold, with average daily surface temperatures of -27°F (-33°C). The present atmosphere of carbon dioxide, with traces of nitrogen, oxygen, water vapor, krypton, and xenon is so thin that daily temperature variations of 180°F (82°C) are common. Temperatures range from -189°F (-123°C) to 63 F (17°C). The first pictures of Mars were taken by Mariner 4 in 1964. Other Mariner flyby missions yielded data in 1969. The first images of its two moons (Phobos, 13 miles or 21 kilometers in diameter, and Deimos, 7.5 miles or 12 kilometers) came from the first Mars orbiter (Mariner 9), launched in 1971. In 1976, two Viking craft landed on the surface. The first craft transmitted data until November 1982, and the second stopped working in April 1980. The Viking orbiters sent information for almost two full Martian years. (Mars takes 1.88 years to orbit the Sun; it turns on its axis once every 24.6 Earth hours.)

Jupiter is the largest of the planets, 1,400 times the volume of Earth but only 318 times the mass, giving it a mean density of about one-fourth that of Earth. Jupiter orbits the Sun in 11.9 Earth years. Its axial rotation is rapid (9.9 hours) and uneven, causing a bulge at its equator. Its hydrogen and helium atmosphere harbors pastel clouds and a Great Red Spot, tinted by compounds consisting of ultraviolet light, lightning, and heat. Its bands indicate atmospheric currents. Jupiter's gravitational field (or magnetosphere) has captured sixteen known moons, the two clusters of Trojan asteroids, and rings of charged particles. Fragments of the comet Shoemaker-Levy 9 (traveling at 130,000 mph or 208,500 km) hit the atmosphere in July 1994, creating explosions and fireballs as large as Earth.

Sixth planet from the Sun, at a mean distance of 888.2 million miles (1,424.6 million kilometers), Saturn revolves around it in 26.446 years. It rotates on its axis every 10.66 hours. Saturn, the second largest planet, with a mass 95.1 times that of Earth, has intricate rings and twenty known satellites, including one with an atmosphere. Titan, The U.S. Pioneer 11 (1979), and Voyagers 1 and 2 (1980 and 1981) have provided extensive information on these and on the planet's atmosphere, 88 percent hydrogen and 11 percent helium. The weight of the atmosphere causes enormous increases in atmospheric pressure. It also causes the condensation of hydrogen gas into liquid and, finally, into metal near the center of the planet. Metallic hydrogen is an electrical conductor forming the basis for Saturn's magnetic field.

Uranus, with a diameter of 32,500 miles

(52,300 kilometers) has a mass 14.5 times greater, a volume 67 times greater, and a gravity 1.17 times greater than Earth. Its magnetic field, one-tenth of Earth's, is sufficient to attract nine rings. Five were discovered in 1977 by the American astronomer James L. Elliot; four more were found by

Voyager 2 in January 1986 which also discovered ten of the planet's fifteen satellites. At a mean distance from the Sun of 1.78 billion miles (2.85 billion kilometers), Uranus takes eighty-four years to orbit it and seventeen hours and fifteen minutes to rotate on its axis. Its atmosphere of hydrogen and helium, with traces of methane, gives it a blue-green color.

Neptune, the eighth planet from the Sun, was discovered in 1846, and was shrouded in mystery until the Voyager 2 fly by in 1989. Its mass is seventeen times that of Earth, and it rotates on its axis every 16.1 hours. Its

The Grand Canyon in the State of Arizona. Erosion has exposed a large number of rock strata, only a very small portion of the Earth's crust.

Rocky desert
in Jordan, strewn with
lava rocks

thick atmosphere of hydrogen, helium, and some methane gives it a bluish color.

Pluto, 1,420 miles (2,280 kilometers) in diameter, was discovered in 1930 by the American astronomer Clyde William Tombaugh on the basis of calculations made in 1905 by the American astronomer Percival Lowell. (Since Pluto's mass seems too small to account for the perturbations of Neptune that Lowell had observed, astronomers are still looking for a tenth planet.) Pluto travels an orbit around the Sun every 247.7 years but rotates on its axis in 6.4 days. Its atmosphere is composed of methane; its temperature range: -369 to -387°F (-223 to -233°C). Pluto's moon, 740

Metamorphic rock consisting
of limestone with veins of calcite.
The original structure of such rock has
changed as a result of extremely high
temperatures or high pressure.

Fossils

Fossils are the hardened remains or imprints of plants or animals of some previous geological period, preserved in rock.

Fossils of partial or complete bodies have been found, usually with hard shells or skeletons. Such fossils were made when the plant or animal was rapidly covered with sediment of some sort (mud or volcanic ash), when it sank (perhaps in a bog), or when it was buried in an earthquake.

Most fossils were formed at the bottom of large lakes, where new layers of sand were repeatedly deposited. Fossils of organisms with soft bodies, like worms or jellyfish, are much less common than those of animals with hard shells or skeletons.

Some fossils were made when the space remaining after the hard parts disappeared was filled by sediment. The body of the plant or animal acted as a mold for the sediment.

Many fossils are simply imprints of plants or animal footprints.

The study of fossils makes it possible to understand evolution and to form a picture of how extinct animals and plants appeared.

Fossil fish
from the Eocene
period

miles (1,190 kilometers) in diameter, was discovered in 1978, orbiting at only about 12,000 miles (19,300 kilometers) from the planet. There is some speculation that Pluto may not be a planet, but a former moon of Uranus.

The Earth
The planet Earth is the third from the Sun in our solar system, at a mean distance of 92.8 million miles (150 million kilometers). It is the fifth largest planet in diameter and the only one known to be capable of supporting life as we know it. Liquid water on its surface and the existence of an atmosphere provide the conditions necessary for life. Water keeps the earth's temperature steady at about -4 to +104°F (-20 to +40°C). The atmosphere moderates the temperature at night and filters out the dangerous UV (ultraviolet) rays of the Sun.

Earth is an imperfect sphere. It is distend-ed 33 feet (10 meters) at the North Pole and 13 miles (21 kilometers) at the equator and depressed about 100 feet (30.5 meters) at the South Pole. The distortions give the planet a slight pear shape.

Plate Tectonics
Earth's crust formed approximately 4.3 million years ago. According to the theory of plate tectonics developed in the twentieth century, the crust is divided into some twelve segments of rock called lithospheric plates. These rest on a soft moving layer called the asthenosphere that flows slowly, expanding unevenly in the heat from the mantle of Earth's score. As the asthenosphere becomes less dense, it rises, causing the plates riding on it to move a few inches (a few centimeters) a year. If great heat lies below an ocean, an oceanic ridge is formed as the crust of Earth is lifted up. The ocean widens as new material from the asthenosphere is added to

Erosion can sometimes lead to the formation of such extremely craggy mountains as the Meteora rocks in northern Greece.

its floor. As this material cools, it sinks, carrying part of the lithosphere with it, in a process called subduction. As the oceanic plates plunge under continental plates, they melt. This molten rock, called magma, may emerge out of volcanoes. Most volcanoes lie along zones of interaction between these plates. As the plates move, they make mountains and cause earthquakes, reshaping Earth's crust. The San Andreas Fault and the earthquakes in California are caused by a Pacific plate butting up against a North American plate.

Continental Drift

The German geophysicist Alfred Wegener first postulated this now widely accepted theory in 1912. It assumes that continents and oceans alike, resting on the plates of the lithosphere, move like pieces of a puzzle. The continents made up the single landmass that has been named Pangaea, 200 million years ago. About 160 million years ago that mass split into Laurasia in the north and Gondwanaland, which moved south. The landmass that would be called India moved north 140 million years ago. Between 120 and 100 million years ago, Australia separated from Antarctica. The American continents and Africa separated between 60 and 40 million years ago. The Atlantic Ocean between them continues to widen.

The Geologic Timescale

Many changes that occurred on the surface of Earth did so in regions that are reasonably accessible to scientists today. Study of rock formations that come from preexisting rocks provides a record of geologic history.

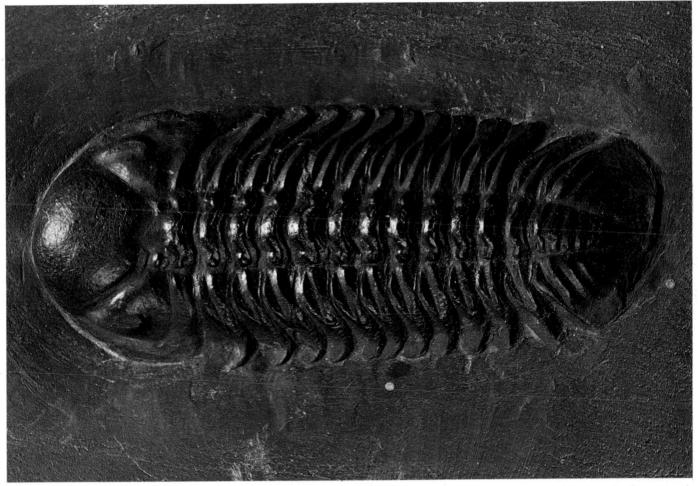

Fossil trilobite. During the Cambrium period the trilobites were the most highly developed animals on Earth: they had a pair of compound eyes and could roll up like hedgehogs to protect themselves.

Igneous rocks, formed by the cooled magma forced onto the surface of Earth, yield information on the planet's past volcanic activity. Metamorphic rocks from deeper in Earth provide a record of plutonism, or magmatic activity. Insight into geologic history is also obtained by comparisons of layers of sedimentary rock formed by erosion and sedimentation.

The formation of Earth's atmosphere, the air surrounding the planet, and the hydrosphere, the water on the planet, set the forces of wind and water in motion, eroding the exposed surface of the planet. The eroded matter (sand, silt, clay) was eventually deposited in lithified (stone) layers. As these layers grew thicker, they grew heavier and were converted to sedimentary rock by cementation, compaction, and induration, or hardening. Any temperature and pressure affecting them was from Earth's surface. Sedimentary rock such as sandstone, made

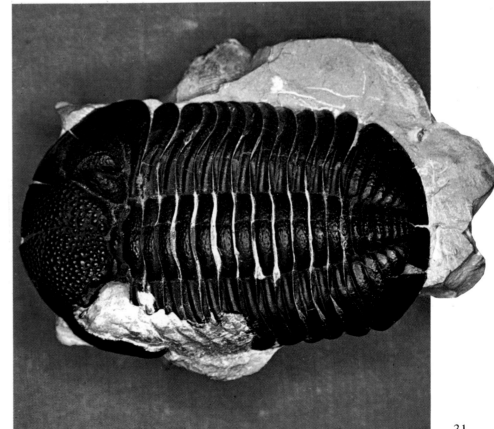

Fossil trilobite
from the Devonian
period

Carboniferous
period fossil with leaves
from a gymnosperm

of quartz sand, and shale, made of clay lies just as it was deposited, miles (kilometers) thick in some areas. Rivers have cut deep canyons through the rock in places like the Grand Canyon of the United States.

Igneous, rather than sedimentary, rock makes up most of the solid mass of Earth. (The term comes from the Latin *igneus*, having to do with fire.) Igneous rock is formed below the planet's surface as molten or partly molten materials cool and harden. Metamorphic rock, distinct from the other two types, is a blend of them. (Metamorphosis means change of shape in Greek.) These rocks have been transformed from preexisting solid rocks by temperature, pressure, and chemical action. They are recrystallized at some depth beneath the surface of Earth. Relatively soft limestone, for example, is hardened (fired by subsurface temperature as if it were clay) into marble; granite is made into gneiss.

In the nineteenth century, scholars posited relative geologic timescales on the basis of events they saw reflected in rock. According to the law of superposition, each successive layer in an undisturbed succession of strata is younger than the ones beneath it. The age of a mountain can thus be ascertained by determining the youngest layers enfolded in an area.

Petrified wood
from the Carboniferous
period discovered
near Glasgow,
Scotland, in 1887

What Is a Dinosaur?

All dinosaurs had the same four characteristics, regardless of any individual variations:

1. All dinosaurs were reptiles.

2. Dinosaurs lived only on land. Flying reptiles (the Pterodactyl and the Quetzalcoatl) and sea reptiles (like the sea lizards Plesiosaur and Ichthygosaur) were not dinosaurs.

3. Dinosaurs lived in the Mesozoic Age. The early reptiles from the Perm Age do not belong in the dinosaur group.

4. Dinosaurs walked upright on pillarlike legs. Lizards and giant crocodiles are not dinosaurs because they crawl; their legs are diagonally attached to their bodies.

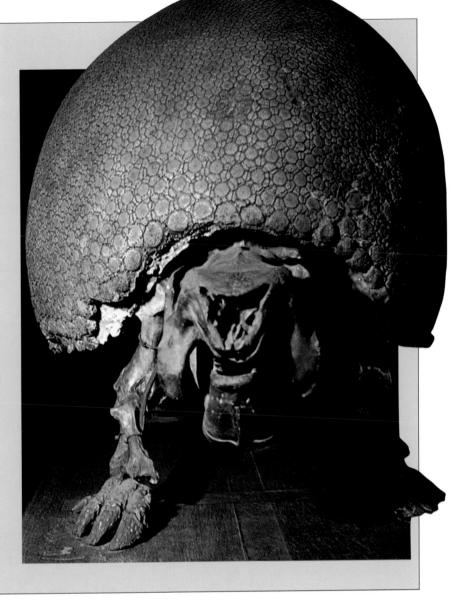

Fossil glyptodon, a giant mammal with typical bony armor from the Quaternary, found on the American continent

Strata were dated absolutely on the basis of the fossils they contained, and virtually no fossils exist from the first 4 to 6 billion years of the planet's history. Only fossils from the past 600 million years have been identified. Geologic study is therefore divided into the Cryptozoic (hidden life) or Precambrian time period and the Phanerozoic (obvious life) or Cambrian period.

A geologic timescale based on sedimentary rock cannot be specific. Scientists, intrigued by the prospect of establishing a more precise time span—a geological yearbook—devised a number of systems to mark off the duration of the geologic periods. However, most of these are now known to have been based on invalid premises.

The discovery of radioactivity in 1896 provided geologists with their long-sought key to accuracy. Radioactivity is a process that takes place at a constant rate. A result of radioactivity is that one chemical element is converted into another or into a different isotope. The speed of the process is discussed in terms of half-life, the time it takes for half the atoms of one element to be converted to the next. Once half-life is known, the age can be calculated based on the ratio between the original element and its end product. Only a few radioactive elements with extremely high half-lives exist in nature.

Geologists realized the great significance of the half-life theory to their field. It enabled them to assign absolute ages, in millions of years, to the divisions of the geologic timescale. They used five elements: thorium-232, uranium-235, uranium-238, potassium-40, and rubidium-87. These convert, respectively, to: lead-208, lead-207, lead-206, argon-40 and calcium-40, and strontium-87.

The oldest dated rocks, which come from Greenland, are over 3,700 million years old, so Earth must be older than that, but how much older could not be ascertained until recently. Scientists began with the concept

33

Cephalopod belonging to the group of mollusks present in large numbers, especially during the Mesozoic era. This type of fossil is called ammonoid.

that Earth as a whole could be viewed as a crystal or a rock sample within a closed system. It was calculated that the three lead isotopes (208, 207, and 206) are the end products of a radioactive series with quite varying half-lives: 14,000, 4,500, and 710 million years, respectively. A fourth lead isotope, lead-204, which is not formed in a radioactive manner, is known. The ratio between the four lead isotopes, therefore, changes over the course of time.

The Age of Earth
Age can be determined by measuring the ratio between certain radioactive isotopes in rocks. Elements with the same number of protons in their nucleus, but a different number of neutrons, are called isotopes of that element. Isotopes possess the same chemical properties. Unstable isotopes eventually fall apart, emitting radioactive rays in a daughter element. Measurement of the ratio of unstable isotope to daughter element gives a good estimate of the age of a rock.

Currently, meteorites are known in which such minimal quantities of thorium and ura-

nium occur that they contain virtually none of the lead caused by radioactive decay: their lead ratio is most likely the same as it originally was. From them scientists concluded that Earth is approximately 4.5 billion years old. Given the fact that all the parts of the solar system must have been created at about the same time, it is interesting that rocks brought back from the Moon by the Apollo astronauts are the same radiometric age, approximately 4.5 billion years, as some meteorites.

Astronomers have also arrived at the conclusion that the Sun must be viewed as a middle-aged star, an estimate that correlates quite well with an Earth age of 4 to 5 billion years.

The Development of Life on Earth
Based on differences seen in the fossil evidence from early, middle, and late Phanerozoic rocks, the development of life on Earth has been divided into three periods: the Paleozoic (ancient life; 600 million years ago), the Mesozoic (middle life; 248 to 66 million years ago), and the Cenozoic (recent life; from 66 million years ago). Within these, time is categorized by worldwide geological periods. These are named for regions where a certain type of rocks predominate. The last two eras of the Cenozoic, called the Tertiary and Quaternary periods, are further subdivided into epochs from the Paleocene to the present Holocene.

Although life is assumed to have existed on Earth for at least 2 billion years, knowledge about the first 1,400 million years is quite incomplete. Even with regard to the last 600 million years, very little is actually known. It is assumed that plants and animals, emerging out of a "primordial ooze," continued to develop into new species. The theory behind this is known as evolution. Though new species are discovered frequently, the number of those species that have existed over the last 600 million years must have

Cenozoic	Quaternary period	1,600,000 years ago
	Tertiary period	65,000,000 years ago
Mesozoic	Cretaceous period	144,000,000 years ago
	Jurassic	208,000,000 years ago
	Trias	245,000,000 years ago
Paleozoic	Permian	286,000,000 years ago
	Carboniferous	360,000,000 years ago
	Devonian	408,000,000 years ago
	Silurian	438,000,000 years ago
	Ordovician	505,000,000 years ago
	Cambrian	570,000,000 years ago
Archean	Precambrian	4,000,000,000 years ago

been many times greater than the 2 million estimated to exist today.

Some 100,000 animal species have been identified from fossils—only a fraction of the number that ever existed—because most animals, even those with skeletons or hard shells, leave little trace of their existence. Even with skeletons and shells, there is a risk of dissolution. Fossils, the hardened remains or imprints of plants and animals preserved in layers of rock, are lost when the rocks break down. Despite this, paleontological excavation and the study of the resultant finds has established an acceptable general outline of the development of life.

The Paleozoic Age

In the Cryptozoic period (from the Greek kryptikos, for hidden), only invertebrate animals lived, leaving scant fossil evidence. The Paleozoic period is distinguished from the Cryptozoic by the evidence of a great variety of animals with a high degree of complexity. Six hundred million years ago only the vertebrates were absent from the animal types present today. The coelenterates (saltwater invertebrates with a large central cavity), mollusks (bivalved animals), arthropods (characterized by jointed legs and bodies), and echinoderms (spiny animals) were all represented. They existed in different species and families than exist today, but nonetheless in the same basic form and organizational structure as their present-day descendants. Only the angiosperms or cryptogams were not yet present in the sometimes great profusion of Paleozoic flora in which relatives of the horsetails and club moss were represented in the form of giant trees. Under favorable conditions—such as during the later Carboniferous era—the wealth of flora resulted in the growth of thick layers of peat from which rich carbon layers and oil developed later on.

In the course of the Ordovician period, the first vertebrate animals evolved from the invertebrates in the form of fish. Vertebrate animals had a structure that represented something completely new amid the great variety of living creatures, since the oldest fish did not possess bony skeletons. Many types of "primordial fish" lacked jaws and were covered—or "armored"—with a kind of bony plate.

A great variety of fish had evolved as early as the Silurian period. By the Devonian period, they were flourishing, and the first land animals, the amphibians, began to develop. These no longer breathed with gills but developed lungs, obtaining their oxygen from air instead of water.

That amphibians still exist today, after so many hundreds of years, indicates that this move to life on land was successful, though amphibians still have to return to water to reproduce. They lay their eggs in water and go through a stage of metamorphosis from gill breathing to lung breathing. An example is the growth of frogs from tadpoles, swim-

ming with tails and possessing gills but no limbs, to adult frogs with lungs and four limbs.

The Mesozoic Age is divided into the Triassic, Jurassic, and Cretaceous periods. During the Mesozoic, flowering plants, birds, and mammals developed, and reptiles evolved from relatively unspecialized amphibians. Reptiles lived entirely on land. Some of them, specifically the dinosaurs, flourished on Earth for 160 million years. They developed into a large number of species, enormously varied in appearance and habit, that spread over every continent. There were herbivores, such as the

Petrified trunk from the Carboniferous period in the Petrified Forest National Park, Arizona

35

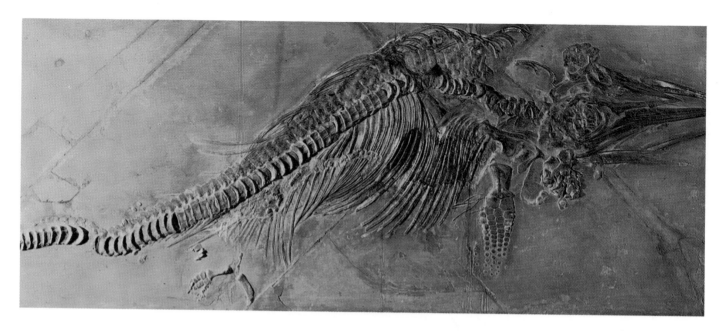

Fossil of an ichthyosaur, an aquatic reptile from the Mesozoic era

Brachiosaurus, and omnivores, scavengers, and predators like the Tyrannosaurus.

Dinosaurs laid their eggs on land rather than in water. These eggs were protected from dehydration by hard, leathery shells. They contained protein that made it possible for the embryo to develop.

Some dinosaurs (like the Hadrosaurus) lived in herds. The Hadrosaurus also protected its young; evidence of its nests has been found in Mongolia.

In some branches of the reptile family, such as the Ichthyosaurus, adaptations to water occurred. These animals retained their typical reptilian structures. Other branches of reptiles took to the air, developing a capacity for flight using skin stretched between the trunk of the body and the extended front legs. One of these, the Quetzal, was as large as a small airplane.

In the Jurassic period, 208 to 144 million years ago, dinosaurs began to develop a

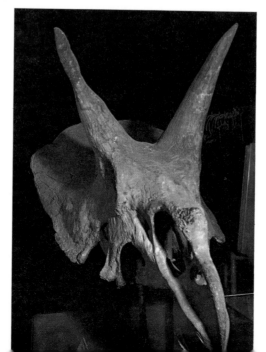

Fossil skull of a *Triceratops calicornis,* a dinosaur from the Cretaceous period, somewhat similar to the present-day rhinoceros

greater ability to fly. They began to grow feathers on the forelegs and other parts of the body. One example of these creatures is the Archaeopteryx.

The absence of evidence of certain species of dinosaur may be explained by the separation of continents from the supercontinent Pangaea.

Sixty-six million years ago the dinosaurs disappeared. The reasons are unknown, though the prevailing view is that a meteorite hit Earth, causing climatic changes to which they could not adapt.

The Dawn of Mammals

At the transition point from the Triassic to the Jurassic periods, reptiles developed the first characteristics that point to the evolution of mammals. Mammals, although certainly primitive, did exist early in the Triassic Age. Very little is known about the history of these primitive Mesozoic mammals. As long as the dinosaurs continued to thrive, the mammals remained an insignificant group.

As the dinosaurs disappeared, the mammals and birds began to flourish, marking the beginning of the Cenozoic Age. Over a relatively short period of time a great variety of animals evolved, some of which exist today.

Among the mammals still living today, three main groups of animals can be classified. The most archaic in evolution are the monotremata, the egg-laying mammals to which the duck-billed platypus and the Australian anteater belong. In the second group, the marsupials, the offspring are born at an early developmental stage. The third and largest group consists of mammals, who share the characteristics of bearing live young.

The glaciated valley of Thures in the Italian Alps. Erosion of the glaciers causes a U-shaped formation of valley.

Human Evolution

Linnaeus and the Immutability of the Species

For a long time scientists assumed that the various species of animals and plants that they knew in their time had all been originally created exactly as they appeared then. The concepts of development and change were alien to them. The Swedish scientist Carolus Linnaeus made a large-scale attempt to bring order to the wealth and variety of living and dead (rocks and minerals) nature in the eighteenth century. He published his results, obtained by extreme scientific precision, in 1735 in his principal work, *Systema naturae*. Apparently, even in the eighteenth

century there were "best-sellers" — the tenth edition of his book appeared in 1758. After more than two centuries, this book is still one of the pillars of systematic zoology.

There were writers as early as the eighteenth century who had begun to question the basic premises of Linnaeus with regard to the immutability of the various species. At the time, their questioning was hardly considered valid. It wasn't until the first half of the nineteenth century that more and more remains of extinct plants and animals were found. The French scholar Baron Georges

Cuvier, who lived from 1769 to 1832, established the sciences of comparative anatomy and paleontology. He contributed to the existing doubts concerning the concept of immutability by discovering and describing fossilized animals. Nonetheless, Cuvier continued to wage a fierce battle against the so-called transformists such as Geoffrey Saint-Hilaire and Lamarck.

In his famous *Discours sur les revolutions de la surface du globe*, Cuvier justified his standpoint by assuming that life on Earth was repeatedly destroyed, only to be re-created over and over.

Darwin's Revolutionary Theory

But in spite of Cuvier's work, the arguments in favor of the gradual evolution of life on Earth became stronger and stronger. Probably no one contributed as much to this thought as Charles Darwin, whose *On the Origin of Species* was published in 1859. No other scientific book has succeeded in creating such excitement, its impact extending far beyond scientific circles. Of course our knowledge in all fields concerned with the question has increased enormously since Darwin wrote the book. Today we know much more about fossilized animals and plants, much more about organic structures and functions, and most of all, much more about the processes of genetics, than did Darwin and his contemporaries. Although Darwin was already convinced of the significance of genetic changes that occur from generation to generation, he was unaware of the specific mechanisms of genetic inheritance.

But for a long time there continued to exist a seemingly irreconcilable gap between minor slow genetic changes and the tremendous rapid changes demonstrated so clearly by fossils. Actually this gap has only been bridged over the last decades. Against a background of the long geologic time span and recent insights into the mechanism of genetics, there can now no longer be any doubt. Genetic changes from generation to generation are sufficiently extensive and account for the long and fascinating history of life on Earth.

Two elements play a dominant role in the history of evolution: chance and necessity. Chance plays an important role because genetic variation occurs at random, permitting an endless number of possibilities. Necessity plays a vital role because variation stems from the ability to adapt to the possibilities offered by nature. Inherent here is an element of selection. From Darwin comes the expression *survival of the fittest*, referring to the survival of those individuals and species that have best adapted to the range of possibilities.

Linnaean Classification

Linnaeus introduced the generic name *Homo* for human. He developed a binary system of classification in which both the name of the genus and the species are used. This system is still used today. The genus is the larger unit of classification; many species can belong to the same genus. The name of the genus is always capitalized; the species name is not. Under this system, *Homo sapiens* (humans capable of thinking) is the name given to modern humans. Earlier evolutionary forms of human are classified in the same genus (*Homo*) but given different species names. The remains of various finds of this early hominid type are classified as *Homo erectus* (erect man) to distinguish them from primates that walked in apelike fashion, using both arms and legs. It is known that *Homo erectus* lived about a half million years ago, probably over quite an extensive area. Humans probably evolved first in Africa, then migrated throughout Europe and Asia, where the first human fossils were found.

The Evolution of *Homo*
The first primates, evolutionary ancestors of humans, appeared in Africa amid the other mammals of the Paleocene period, some 65 million years ago. They were small ground-dwelling animals, not much bigger than a mouse. Although exclusively insect-eaters, they already showed characteristics that would later appear in more developed primates. As they evolved, they moved from the ground to trees. They adapted to climbing and eating fruit.

The larger prosimians (half-apes) seem to have evolved from these first primates in the Eocene epoch. Developing strongly over the Oligocene epoch (about 40 million years ago), they began to differentiate from the apes. This is evident from fossils of the small ape, *Oligopithecus,* found in the Fayum depression in Egypt. Its name is derived from the Greek words *oligos* (small) and *pithekos* (ape). From a number of other scanty sources, their development can be linked to the *Dryopithecus.* These tree apes (from *dryo,* tree) lived at the beginning of the Miocene epoch, approximately 13 million years ago.

There is reason to assume that their development represented a critical phase in primate history. Here a difference in development occurred that would lead to the chimpanzee, the gorilla, and their next of kin, the human being.

In Egypt, earlier traces have been found of a slightly different but developmentally related ape, *Aegyptopithecus* (Egyptian ape). Older than the *Dryopithecus,* it has left few remains behind. Scholars have long puzzled over the question of why primate fossils are so extremely scarce in comparison to those of many other groups of mammals. The reason is thought to be the adaptation of the primates to life in the trees. The remains of animals living along lakeshores or riverbanks had a much greater chance of being covered by sediment.

Increasing Specialization
The evolution of the primate is characterized primarily by the development of the brain. Scholars have hypothesized that the impetus to this brain development was given by life in trees. Other important properties that developed in primates are clearly linked to their arboreal life. Their stereoscopic vision improved, with powerful, forward-facing eyes. Their hands developed for grasping branches, using four agile fingers and a prehensile thumb. For such a lifestyle a finely developed brain with quick reaction capability was a great advantage. Brain development is seen in other groups of mammals, as well, but nowhere as early and to the degree of development of the primates.

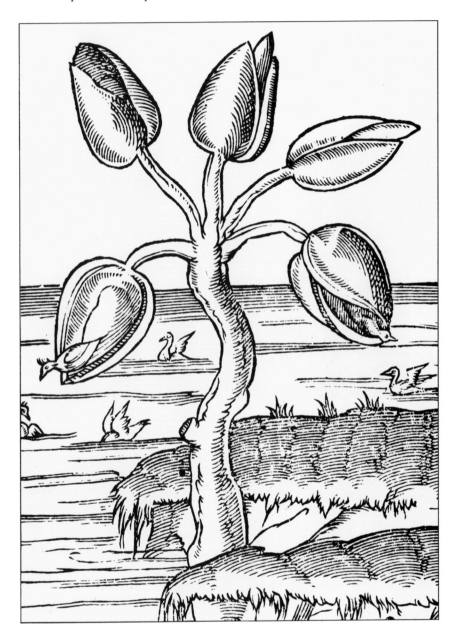

Other developmental characteristics include a shortening of the jaws (with a reduction in the number of teeth), decrease in the sense of smell, and a slow development of the young after birth. Ape faces came to lie beneath rather than in front of the cranial cavity. Due to its diversity, the group as a whole is not easy to characterize.

The development of mental capacity in humans would reach an especially high level of specialization, a new element in the evolution of life. The direct predecessor of humans, the *Australopithecus,* lived late in

Aristotles' theory of spontaneous reproduction was the inspiration for this thirteenth-century illustration showing trees producing geese.

39

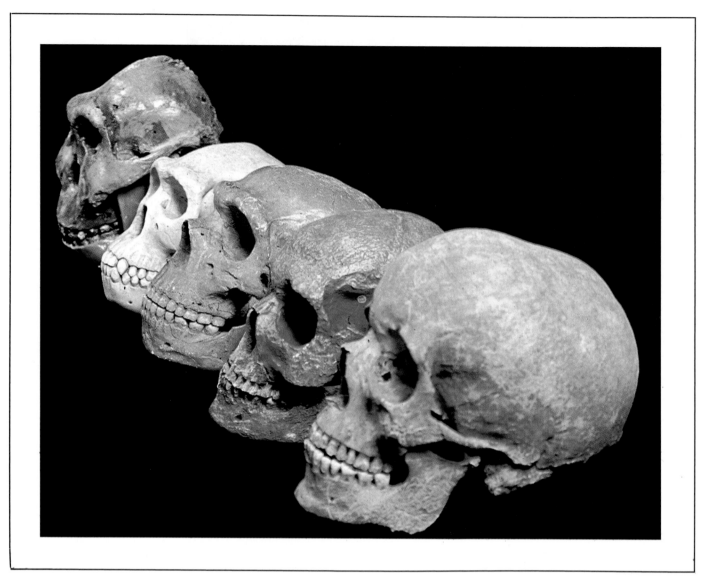

The development
of the hominoid. *From left to right:*
Hominoid from Olduvai
(1,500,000 to
2,000,000 years ago),
Java (250,000 years ago),
the Neandertal (500,000
years ago),
Anatomically Modern
Humans
(30,000 years ago) and
modern man (Roman-British)
c.500 AD.

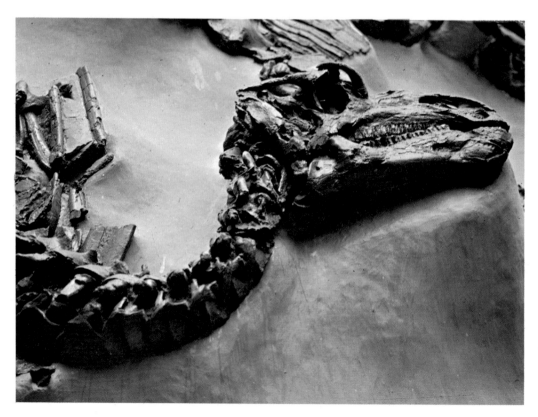

Fossil skeleton of an
iguanodon, a very large
reptile from the Cretaceous
period

the Cenozoic (Late Miocene) Age, approximately 5 million years ago. This period was characterized by the relatively short but intense changes in the climate of the Ice Age. The development of the human branch of the primates coincided with these climatologic shifts. The latest and most decisive phase in human development is difficult to separate from the immense backdrop of the Ice Age.

The Ice Age

Borders of stone and gravel, called moraines, edge the front and sides of most glaciers. Analysis of the moraines of the Alps shows that they were transported from Scandinavia by an enormous ice cap that covered Europe, extending from England to Poland. In North America, an ice cap extended even farther south, covering not only what is now Canada, but the northern portion of the present United States. Compared to these, the present-day ice caps that cover most of Greenland and Antarctica are quite small.

Several periods of glacier cover (called glacials) have been recognized. From the evidence of fossilized plant remains found between the moraines of glaciers, the climate in the interglacial periods, when the great masses of ice retreated, was mild, perhaps even warmer than Earth today.

The great ice caps of Europe and North America were created by drastic changes in the worldwide climate. The temperature, influenced by the fluctuation of the Gulf Stream, dropped gradually. (Normally steady, ocean streams are great currents of warm water in the ocean that affect the temperature of both the surrounding seas and the air above them.) As the ice caps grew, they themselves influenced the climate. Measured in geologic time, the Ice Ages lasted only a short duration. However, the recurring advance and retreat of the ice had a profound effect on the appearance of Earth. The climate changes induced by the glaciers were not limited to those areas directly inundated by them. The present belt of desert across North Africa and the Middle East received a much greater amount of precipitation in the Ice Ages. Rainy periods, called pluvials, can be differentiated from drier periods, called interpluvials. These correspond to the glacials and interglacials of the more northerly areas.

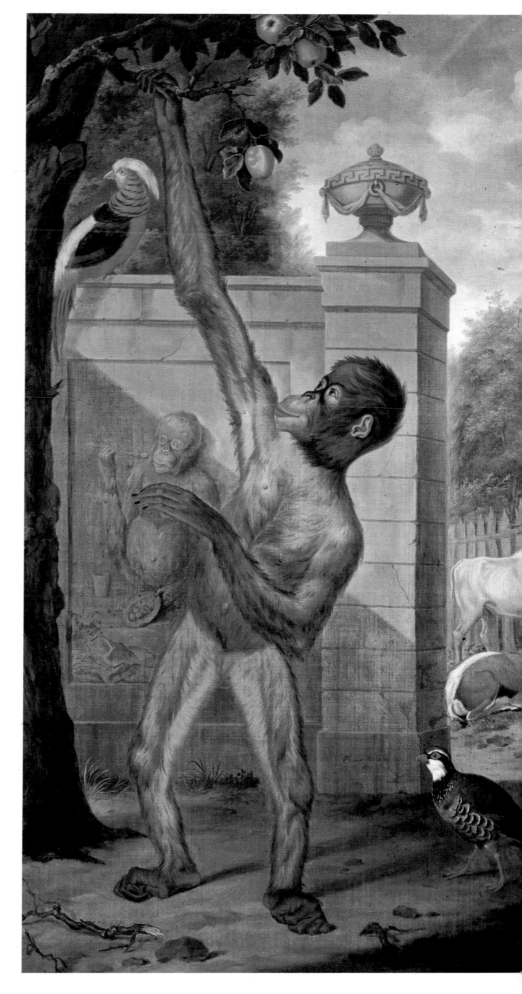

Cartoon illustrating Darwin's theory: the ape misbehaving in the ancestral garden

Across Earth, zones of vegetation shifted. In Europe, plants and animals were caught in an interglacial climate between two constantly growing ice caps. Several interglacial periods can be identified by the presence or absence of certain plant varieties. Animals either had to change their habitat or adapt to it.

The harsh cold that, geologically speaking, "suddenly" enveloped Earth, set in motion an evolutionary process of adaptation. New types of mammal, such as woolly mammoths and rhinoceroses, appeared with acquired characteristics that enabled them to survive the icy climate. The giant woolly mammoth is a spectacular example. It evolved from the elephant, normally a dweller of warm climates.

Another significant effect of the enormous glacier buildup was a drop in the sea level. The water that fed the glaciers in the form of snow and ice was drawn from the huge reservoir of the ocean, lowering it some 150 to 200 feet (45 to 60 meters) below its present level. As a consequence, many shallow seas dried up completely, including the North Sea, the plateau between the Sunda Islands in Indonesia and the Bering Strait between Russia and Alaska.

It is quite conceivable that constant fluctuations in climate, with all the associated effects upon the environment, had particular influence on human evolution.

Methods of Dating

Until the discovery of radioactivity in the twentieth century, the age of Earth could not be calculated except by the relative scale of geologic time. With the application of radioactive dating to geologic time, an absolute scale could be devised.

In the last few decades, understanding of the development of Earth and life on it has greatly increased. There is new evidence of climatic changes taken from peat bogs and lake bottom deposits. Plants react particularly acutely to climatic shifts. Pollen grains, microscopically small and well encapsulated, can function as annual records of even the most minimal changes. This is also true of the remains of one-celled ocean animals, absorbed into the mire of the ocean floor. These provide a picture of the temperature changes of the seawater. The great advantage of the new techniques is that they make it possible to ascertain both major and minor fluctuations across the whole Earth. Before them, information came almost entirely from the tracing of glacier formation. This confined our knowledge to the larger fluctuations and the moderate regions of the Northern Hemisphere.

Reconstruction drawing of the mammoth, which was covered with a long woolly coat. A few specimens of these contemporaries of Paleolithic humans were found, still completely intact, in the frozen ground of Siberia.

Reconstruction of Pithecanthropus erectus, based on discoveries f ound near Trinil on Java

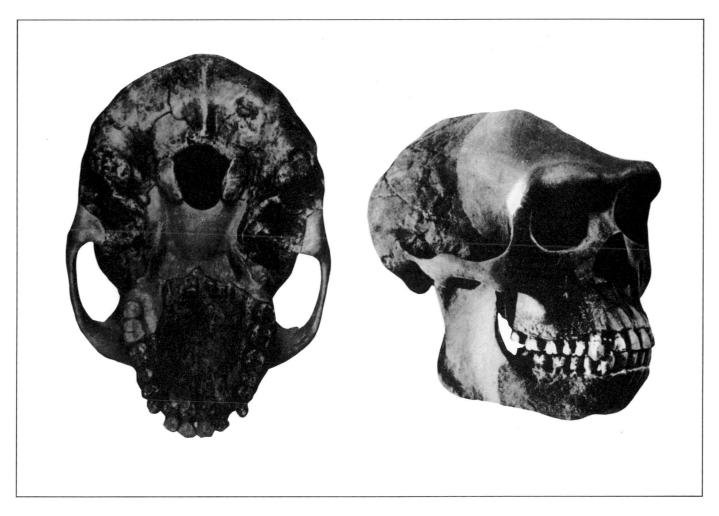

The C14 Method

The best-known element used in the classification process is C14, a radioactive isotope of carbon. As it spreads through the atmosphere, C14 is absorbed by plants and, by way of those plants, ends up in animals. Hence, there is a small amount of C14 present in all organisms.

After organisms die, something remains, whether it be the fibrous matter of plants or the shells and bones of animals. Radioactive deterioration continues, but no more absorption can take place in the dead organism. The degree to which the C14 has deteriorated after the organism's death reveals the age of the organism.

The C14 dating method has produced highly useful results, especially in the analysis of the prehistoric periods.

One problem with the C14 method, however, is that its dates are only accurate within a standard deviation, which can be a range of many years. Another method, called dendrochronology, is as old as the C14 method and can be used to calibrate such deviation. Dendrochronology is the comparison of the annual rings of trees that died or were cut down at different times in the past. For every year that it lives, a tree develops a new layer or ring of growth between its outer bark and the layer of the previous year's growth. In cross-section, these rings are concentric circles, with the earliest growth at the center heartwood (the older, more durable, central wood of trees). The method makes it possible to ascertain the year a tree fell, dating back to approximately 6000 BC.

In addition to the C14 method and dendrochronology, scientists today have other tools for ascertaining past geologic dates. They use the presence of radioactive isotopes in deposits on the ocean floor and the presence of light and heavy oxygen isotopes in polar ice. Over recent years, studies have also been made of reversions in Earth's magnetic field. Evidence that the North and South Poles trade places can be found in magnetic rocks.

These and other scientific methods and insights have significantly broadened our understanding of the most recent geologic history of Earth. It appears, on the evidence from ice formations alone, that the number of climatic changes was greater than originally thought. In addition, it appears that these climatic shifts extended over a much longer period than the formation of glaciers indicated. These new insights make a precise definition of "ice age" a difficult matter. Geologists prefer to use the term

Upper part of the skull of Homo erectus remains from Java, seen from beneath the skull, and a reconstruction of the entire skull

43

Reconstruction of
Homo erectus remains
from China
("Peking man")

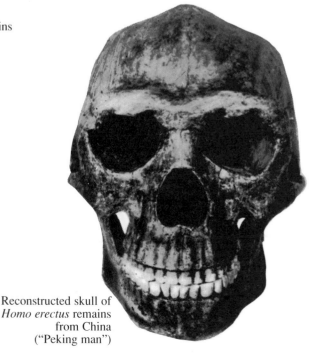

Reconstructed skull of
Homo erectus remains
from China
("Peking man")

Pleistocene, which fits both in form and interpretation with the other subdivisions of the Cenozoic period.

The Missing Link

In 1887, Eugene Dubois went to Sumatra as a health official. He went not only with the intention of taking care of the soldiers there but with the hope of uncovering the legendary "missing link," the missing connection between man and ape. He spent four years intensively hunting for clues on this quest. In 1894 he found a fossilized humanlike thighbone and a fragment of the crown of a skull near the village of Trinil in central Java. The remains of other animals he saw in the same area confirmed to him that the discovery was very old. The shape of the thighbone indicated to Dubois that its owner must have walked upright. The fragment of the skull led him to conclude that the primate's brain volume must have been approximately 61 in³ (1,000 cm³), a volume between that of the species anthropoid (higher primates), 31 in³ cubic inches (500 cm³), and present-day man, 82 in³ (1,350 cm³). Two years after his 1894 discovery, Dubois published a description of his findings. He named his creature (now classified as a type of *Homo erectus*) *Pithecanthropus erectus* (upright anthropoid).

Although the notion of a "missing link" today has changed radically from what it was a hundred years ago, the enormous scientific value of Dubois's discovery is beyond question. It led, at that time, to heated discussions among proponents and opponents of his theory. It is far easier now than then to establish the geologic age of fossils. After World War II, G. H. R. Von Koenigswald collected much new material in Java. He came to the conclusion that the *Pithecanthropus* must have lived only some 500,000 to 600,000 years ago, not long enough to provide an evolutionary link to modern man.

Discoveries in China

New discoveries were unearthed in China, where Davidson Black found a fossilized human molar at a site outside Peking in 1927. In the 1930s, various investigators, including Franz Weidenreich and Pierre Teilhard de Chardin, worked in China with considerable success. Thanks to their systematic excavations of well-chosen sites, quite a few fossilized remains were brought to light.

These findings enabled scholars to form a picture of *Sinanthropus pelanensis* (Peking man), as the newly discovered find was named. This type of *Homo erectus* must have lived 400,000 to 200,000 years ago, a little later than the *Pithecanthropus* found by

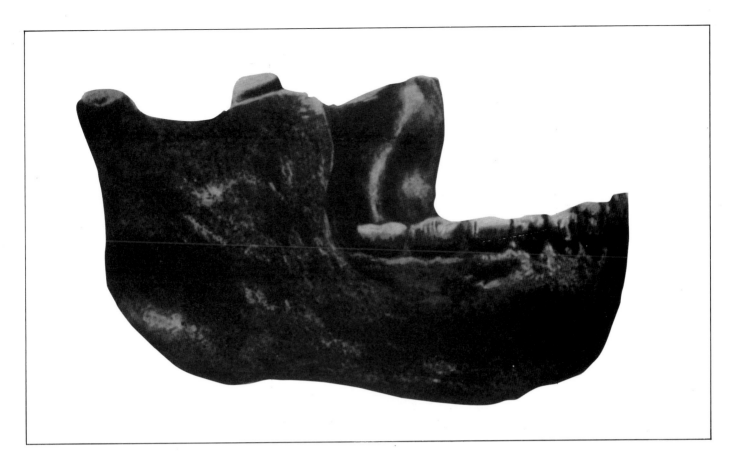

Lower jaw of
Homo erectus remains from
Heidelberg, found near
Mauer, Germany,
in 1907

Dubois. There is evidence that these examples of the species hunted and used fire.

Peking man is a collective term referring to six virtually complete skullcaps and facial fragments, fourteen cranial parts, fifteen jawbones, 157 teeth, one collarbone, three humerous bones, seven femurs, one shinbone, and one wrist. These came from some forty individual males and females of varied age. Excavations where the bones were found seventy years ago in the caves of Zhoukoudian, 30 miles (48 kilometers) south of Beijing, have not been completed. According to an article in the *New York Times* (December 23, 1995), much of the earlier work was lost or destroyed, a casualty of World War II. Two crates of bones, sent out from China for safekeeping, were seized and destroyed by the Japanese. Unfortunately, today most of the remaining findings are stored, unidentified, with thousands of animal bones from the same digs. The tagging system was lost in the political disarray of modern China, especially the "Ten Years of Chaos" (1966–1976) with its purging of anything from ancient China.

European Findings

In Europe, thus far, only one fragment has been found that may be considered to represent any type of *Homo erectus*. This is the jaw from Heidelberg, Germany, found in the Günz-Mindel interglacial. The fragment dates from about 700,000 years ago. All other findings of the *Homo* genus in Europe are considered to belong in the early *Homo sapiens* group that began to develop some 200,000 years ago.

The skulls from Ehringsdorf, Steinheim, and Swanscombe are of interest because of their great geologic age, particularly the latter. The Swanscombe skull was found, along with tools ascribed to the Acheulian culture, in terrace deposits from the Thames. It indicates that *Homo sapiens* had already been present in Europe for a few hundred thousand years. For a long time Swanscombe's findings went uncorroborated by others. The Hungarian scholar Vertesszollos recorded a description of human remains probably even older than the Swanscombe skull. Dating from the last part of the Mindel ice age, these remains are also of a *Homo sapiens* type, although certain parts of them show similarities to the *Homo erectus*.

Archaic *Homo sapiens*

Most findings of fossilized human remains in Europe—and there are quite a few—originate from deposits associated with the last Ice Age. These specimens can be classified into two groups, once referred to as the Neandertal and the Cro-Magnon types. In today's terminology, *Homo sapiens* is further classified as archaic and modern man (*Homo sapiens sapiens*). Neandertals hold a remarkable place among types of humans. Certain characteristics of its skeleton appear more

45

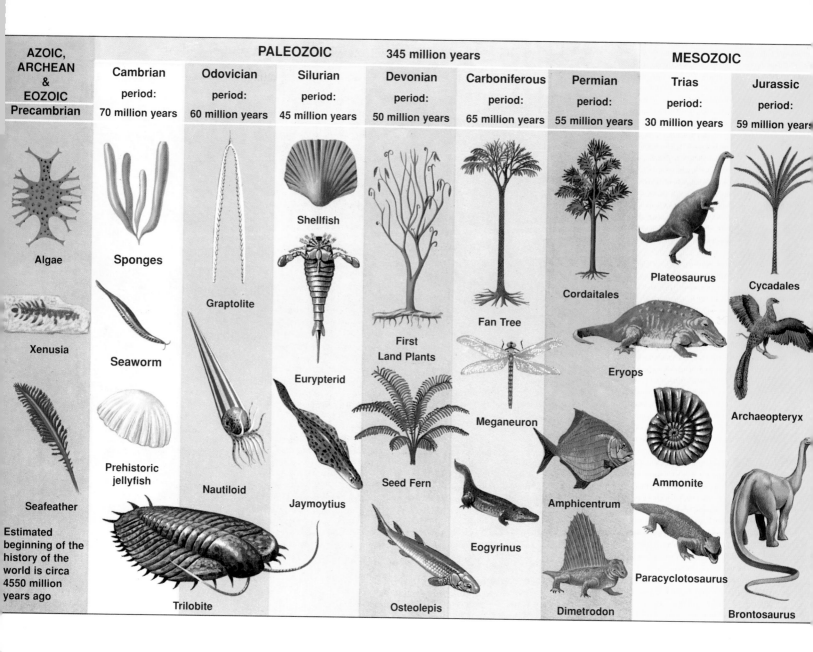

AZOIC, ARCHEAN & EOZOIC Precambrian	PALEOZOIC 345 million years						MESOZOIC	
	Cambrian period: 70 million years	Odovician period: 60 million years	Silurian period: 45 million years	Devonian period: 50 million years	Carboniferous period: 65 million years	Permian period: 55 million years	Trias period: 30 million years	Jurassic period: 59 million years

Algae

Xenusia

Seafeather

Estimated beginning of the history of the world is circa 4550 million years ago

Sponges

Seaworm

Prehistoric jellyfish

Graptolite

Nautiloid

Trilobite

Shellfish

Eurypterid

Jaymoytius

First Land Plants

Seed Fern

Osteolepis

Fan Tree

Meganeuron

Eogyrinus

Amphicentrum

Dimetrodon

Cordaitales

Eryops

Ammonite

Paracyclotosaurus

Plateosaurus

Cycadales

Archaeopteryx

Brontosaurus

Time Scale
of the History
of Earth

primitive than that of modern humans. Nonetheless, since *Homo sapiens* appeared earlier, Neandertals cannot be viewed as an evolutionary forerunner of modern humans.

Neandertal remains have been known for quite some time and their name is taken from the picturesque Neander Valley between Elberfeld and Düsseldorf in Germany, where an incomplete skeleton was found in a small cave in 1856. (The silent *h* in *thal* [valley] has been dropped in modern German. Some scientists still prefer the original spelling, Neanderthal.)

The species probably adapted for survival in a cold climate. At the beginning of the last Ice Age, Neandertals ranged over an extensive area. Their remains have been found in France, Italy, Gibraltar, the former Yugoslavia, Israel, Rhodesia, South Africa, and western Asia. (The American continents

were apparently not yet populated.) Their development occurred approximately 180,000 to 30,000 years before our era. Neandertals are usually regarded as representatives of a decreasingly unsuccessful side branch in human evolution. It is not clear why they disappeared.

Modern *Homo*

The *Homo sapiens* skeleton, differing anatomically in no pivotal way from that of the modern human, is significantly unlike that of the more heavily built Neandertal. *Homo sapiens* have been dated at 200,000 years ago. Early modern humans lived in Europe in the second part of the last Ice Age, spreading gradually throughout the rest of the world. The most remarkable evidence of their presence lies in the spectacular paintings found in the caves of southwest France and northern Spain.

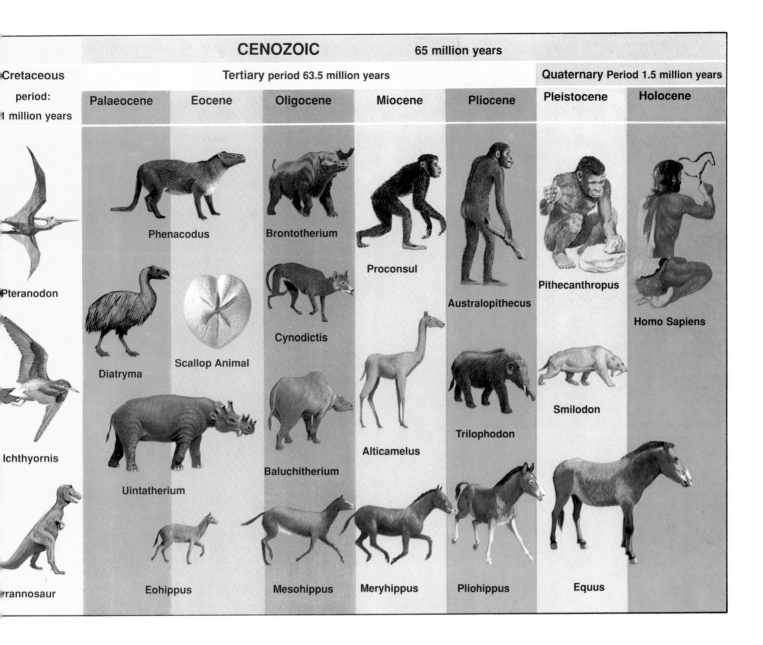

	CENOZOIC				65 million years		

Cretaceous period: 1 million years	Tertiary period 63.5 million years					Quaternary Period 1.5 million years	
	Palaeocene	Eocene	Oligocene	Miocene	Pliocene	Pleistocene	Holocene

Pteranodon

Ichthyornis

Tyrannosaur

Phenacodus

Diatryma

Scallop Animal

Uintatherium

Eohippus

Brontotherium

Cynodictis

Baluchitherium

Mesohippus

Proconsul

Alticamelus

Meryhippus

Australopithecus

Trilophodon

Pliohippus

Pithecanthropus

Smilodon

Equus

Homo Sapiens

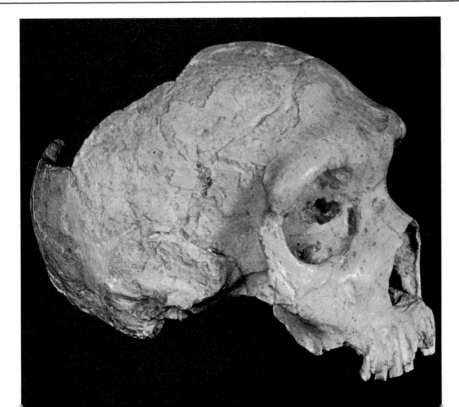

African Findings

The early findings of fossilized human remains in Java and China seemed to point to the idea that humans originated in Asia, but this is no longer the understanding. They probably originated in Africa. A relatively clear sequence of successive humanlike creatures, up to and including *Homo sapiens,* has been found in this part of the world. These findings began with a remarkable discovery by Raymond Dart near Taung in South African 1924: a child's skull. The fact that no adult skull had been discovered made comparison with other findings more difficult. Still, it is definite that the skull retained a more primitive set of characteristics than

Skull of a Neandertal, found in Gibraltar, Spain

Reconstruction of
a Neandertal

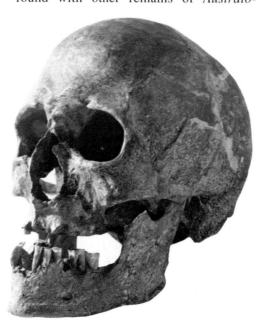

Skull of
Chancelade human,
belonging
to Anatomically Modern
Humans

pithecus indicates that this species must have lived on Earth much earlier than did the *Pithecanthropus*, probably a bit more than 4 million years ago.

The work of Mary and Louis Leakey in northeast Africa is of particular importance, beginning with their findings in 1959 in the Olduvai Gorge of Tanzania. Their meticulous investigation, continued by their son Richard and his wife, Meave, has provided significant finds. The Leakeys have been able to differentiate various types of anthropoids. These included a number of types of *Australopithecus;* his successor, *Homo habilis*; and, finally, *Homo erectus*. These finds point to the significance of Africa in the history of human evolution.

There is enough evidence to assume that, after the Oligocene epoch, three separate lines in the evolution of the anthropoids ("manlike" or higher primates) branched off. (The gibbons and orangutans branched off from the main line earlier.) These three parallel branches evolved into the gorilla, the chimpanzee, and the human being.

Aegyptopithecines, some 35 million years ago, began to evolve into *Proconsulids* (existing between 22 and 14 million years ago). Future finds will certainly shed more light upon the history of evolution and the role of *Kenyapithecus* (living about 14 million years ago). African finds have contributed more to the pre-*Australopithecus* history of the hominids (humans and their direct predecessors) than those from any other continent, with the most important material coming from Kenya. Finds dated from the Miocene epoch are attributed to *Proconsulids*. Hundreds of examples of this hominid are now known, subdivided into three different types. They all show—particularly in the structure of their skulls—anatomic characteristics that do not appear in the larger apes. These characteristics, however, do appear in *Australopithecines*, in *Homo erectus*, and in *Homo sapiens*. There is general consensus among scholars on the inclusion of *Proconsulids* with the hominids. This fills a big gap in our knowledge of the past. It means that the history of the human being can be traced back to the Miocene epoch, and perhaps even farther, into the Oligocene.

Much remains to be explained, given present knowledge of the overall pattern of human evolution. Large parts of Africa have been studied only minimally or not at all.

the *Pithecanthropus* of Java. Even so, the African fragment already exhibited a number of humanlike characteristics. Dart gave it the name *Australopithecus africanus*. Today, much more material of this and related types is available. The fauna (or animal evidence) found with other remains of *Australo-*

48

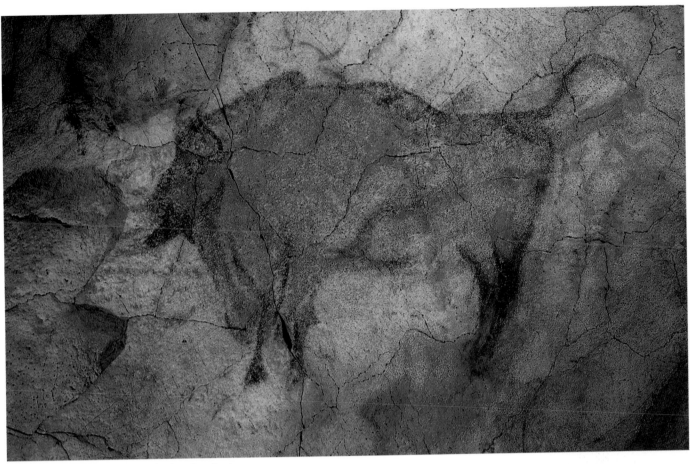

Bison. Painting in the caves of Altamira, Spain

The Paleolithic

Humans Begin Using Stone Tools

The archaeological record of humans begins with their first use of tools. The forerunners of present-day humans are categorized as human when they can be connected with tools that they have used. Humans developed as tool-users in the Paleolithic period, which takes its name from *paleo* (old) and *lithos* (stone). Archaeologists call such human-made items "artifacts," referring to "artificially made objects." Actually this scientific name is more correct than the specification "tools." The term *artifact* also covers finds that are not tools. (Animals do not generally make tools, although some types of birds and many primates use sticks or stones. Chimpanzees are known to make and use tools for specific purposes.)

On the basis of skeletal morphology (the characteristic shapes of skeletons), two types

of human beings have been identified as living in the Paleolithic. Based on sporadic finds of parts of early human skeletons dating from the Ice Age, these are identified as Neandertals and anatomically modern humans (AMHs).

Archaeologists have recovered flint tools that must have been made by Neandertals, prehistoric hominids adapted to life in very cold conditions. When we consider that our history has lasted a few thousand years, the Neandertal era seems incredibly long ago.

Neandertals retained a number of characteristic traits from their own evolutionary ancestors. These included a long skull ending in a point at the back of the head, a lower jaw with barely any chin, and a very low brainpan. The eyebrow ridges were very pronounced and joined. The arms were longer in

Flint bifacial axe
from the Acheulian
period

comparison to the legs than ours are today, but the notion that Neandertals walked bent over has turned out to be erroneous. Even earlier types of humans walked upright.

Parts of human skeletons dating from the Ice Age have been found all over Europe. These are *Homo sapiens,* clearly different from the Neandertals and identical to modern humans. These skeletons are characterized by a well-developed skull, a high forehead, somewhat square eye sockets, and a pronounced chin. *Homo sapiens* supplanted Neandertals approximately 30,000 years ago, over a relatively short period of time. In the course of a few thousand years, Neandertals died out. How much *Homo sapiens* had to do with this remains, for the time being, unknown.

Modern humans have existed for at least 200,000 years. Like Neandertals, early anatomically modern humans could keep themselves alive under severe weather conditions. In the subarctic tundra of today, people are as migratory as their ancestors, establishing no permanent residence and living by hunting and collecting food. This lifestyle is characteristic of the Paleolithic. They hunted large animals like the mammoth and the woolly rhinoceros with spear and harpoon and, later, with bow and arrow. The modern counterpart still hunts sea mammals (whales and seals), reindeer, and smaller animals like the polar hare. Like their predecessors, modern humans collect berries and a variety of plants. During short interglacials, early humans fished, as well, using harpoons and hooks made of bone. Tools were made of wood, bone, antler, and flint. Since organic material often rots, great attention has been paid to flint. Periods of history have been

designated according to corresponding flint processing techniques.

Flint Processing

The various developmental stages of stone processing have made it possible to divide the Stone Age into various periods: the old, the middle, and the new stone age (the Paleolithic, the Mesolithic, and the Neolithic). These periods are again subdivided into lower, middle, and upper. For example, the Mousterian culture of the Neandertal falls in the Middle Paleolithic.

The Old Stone Age has been designated as the period from the appearance of the first human beings, 2.5 million years ago, to about 10,000 BC. Various cultural streams are differentiated on the basis of the tools used and the technology applied at various times during these Paleolithic periods. The first hominid species to make tools is called *Homo habilis.* The lower Paleolithic is characterized by roughly constructed tools. These were usually made of flint, which occurred mainly in areas of calcium and chalk deposits. Flint is very hard if hit directly but chips relatively easily if hit at an angle. Paleolithic people, like contemporary craftspeople of the Americas and Oceania, used palm-long rounded rocks for chipping sharp flint edges for spear points and arrowheads. Softer material like antler for retouching the stone has been used by both as well.

Acheulean Culture

The most significant tool from the lower Paleolithic period is the hand ax. This was an extremely simple tool, a piece of rock randomly chipped to provide a sharp edge. A celt, on the other hand, was a tool deliberately chiseled on one or two sides to create an actual edge that roughly compares to that of a chisel or an ax head. (Chisels are flat on one side, beveled on the other; axes and knives have V-shaped blades.) Hand axes were held in the hand and used to butcher animals and to chop or carve wood. The Paleolithic culture that originally developed them is called the Acheulean.

The first hand axes were discovered near the North African town of Abbeville. The culture, an offshoot of the Acheulean, has been named after the nearby town. (Nearly all discovered Paleolithic cultures were named after the French towns nearest the findings.) Since the middle of the last century, extensive investigations have been carried out there by French archaeologists.

The axes of the Abbeville area are rather blunt, although they show definite advances over the simple chopper in the technique of stone processing. Made from chunks of flint, they were chipped to the shape of a flattened pear. The narrow upper part (or grip) was often left in its natural state. The blade, chipped to form an edge, is irregular.

It is generally assumed that the Acheulean culture dates back to the beginning of the second interglacial (the Mindel-Riss interglacial), approximately 400,000 years ago. According to some scholars, this culture is even older. Most datings of such early periods can be nothing more than estimates. The presence of the hand ax, however, is a reliable indicator of the presence of humans: it cannot occur by chance.

New Techniques

Over the Acheulean period (1.5 million years ago to 200,000 years ago), hand axes were made smaller and more varied in shape (triangular or oval). People also began to use many other stone tools. Both core tools and flake tools were made. Flake tools were created from the chips that were broken off stone. Such chips are termed *blades* if the piece is about twice as long as it is wide. There are primitive examples of this simple industry among the earliest people of Asia. In the past, archaeologists attempted to differentiate between the two different technical traditions (the core and the broken-off), but such a division proved impossible. The traditions overlap in both time and culture. Within various Paleolithic cultures, both core and flake tools have been found. Core axes and the flakes broken off them to be made into other tools have even been discovered together.

Flint scrapers from
the Magdalenian period,
c.15,000 BC

Flint hand axes
from the Lower Paleolithic
period

The knapping technique (meaning to break with a quick blow) was improved, as time went on, through use of what has been named the Levallois technique, whereby the flint chunk was flattened on one side and rounded off on the other to make a sturdy, sharp-scraping tool that could be detached from the core by a single well-placed blow. Originally thought to characterize a single culture, this technique proved to be utilized in various societies. The shape of these core tools was carefully planned. The single edge

in addition to a few tools of bone. They are particularly known for their double-edged knives but they also produced various types of small axes and denticulate (saw-toothed) tools. Most of these objects were undoubtedly used in skinning and cleaning the animals they killed and in working with bones and wood.

Cultures with uniquely Mousterian characteristics existed for at least 50,000 years. They have been found in Europe, North Africa, Asia, and Malaysia. The most significant exception is the part of Africa south of the Sahara Desert. This great barrier occurred during the third interglacial period, when Africa experienced an extensive period of drought.

For a long time scholars thought that Mousterian culture was unique to the Neandertals, but evidence exists to the contrary. It is quite certain that *Homo sapiens* had already existed before the advent of the Neandertals. Their skeletons have been found in Mousterian layers.

In most places the tools have been found together with the remains of Neandertals, as they were in France, Germany, Belgium, and Spain. The European findings have been discovered in open-air sites as well as in caves and under the shelters of overhanging cliffs.

A stag hit
by many arrows.
Painting in the cave
of Candamo

was sharpened with tiny blows, a process called retouching. The new method was particularly efficient because it used virtually all of the core.

Middle Paleolithic

The Levallois technique was first used during the third interglacial, about 200,000 years ago. The Middle Paleolithic starts at this time and is distinguished from the preceding era by this and other techniques of stone processing. It was during this period that the Neandertals appeared.

In the Middle Paleolithic Age people succeeded in considerably increasing their range of tools and equipment. The Mousterians made the stone scrapers with one sharp side,

The Venus of Laussel
(Dordogne, France), female
figure engraved in stone.
In her hand she has a bison horn,
as a fertility symbol. Dating
from the Aurignacian/Gravettian
period, c. 23,000 BC.

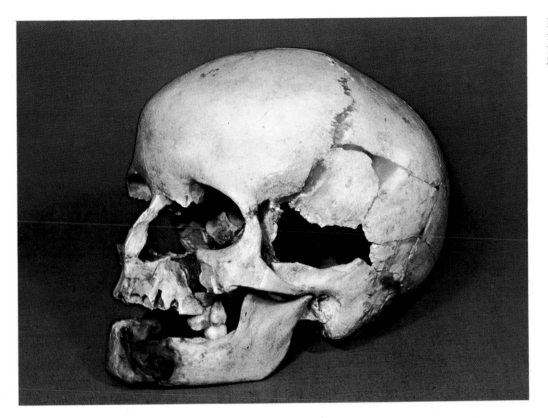

These offered natural protection from the harsh climate of the Ice Age.

Social Organization

Traces of temporary Neandertal shelters located in the open air have been discovered. These were probably circular, hutlike structures constructed of hanging hides. Neandertals may have scraped hides clean and used them for bedding, clothing, and pouches, as well as tents. There is no evidence that they tanned leather. Fireplaces reveal that by this time fire, known since the Lower Paleolithic Age, was in common use for cooking and heat.

The size of most of the animals hunted by early humans would seem to have required some degree of cooperation and social organization. Undoubtedly the people of this era hunted in groups. They also scavenged animals that had died naturally or had been killed by other predators. Fruits, plants, herbs, and fish were also consumed, and perhaps humans as well. There is highly contested evidence of Neandertal cannibalism.

Some concept of an afterlife existed, given the few very well-cared-for graves that have been found. The deceased were sprinkled with red ocher and buried with their tools, perhaps suggesting belief that the dead had further use for them.

The last traces of the Neandertals date from approximately 30,000 years ago, the middle of the last Ice Age. The cultures of the Upper Paleolithic Age belong to the *Homo sapiens* group. Once again, most evidence has been found in France, where both the climate and the many caves offered great opportunity for human survival. (Two other factors play a role here: French sites are accessible today and they allowed for the significant preservation of ancient remains.)

Refinement and Specialization

Cultural innovations at the start of the Upper Paleolithic are remarkable. Stone processing was further developed. Tools exhibited an increasing degree of specialization. A single tool was no longer made to serve a wide variety of purposes. Specialized tools were created and designed to serve specific purposes. A wide variety of stone scrapers, knives, files, and pointed tools (called burins and borers) have been recovered from this era. In addition, there are tools made of bone, ivory, and antler. These had probably been made in earlier periods, but clear archaeological evidence has been found only from this period. The technique used in these materials is sometimes so complex that some scholars claim them to be the work of specialized craftsmen. According to other scholars, however, such true specialists were not present until the Mesolithic period, which commenced at around 10,000 to 7,000 years ago.

The Upper Paleolithic covers roughly the time from 40,000 to 10,000 years ago. It is generally divided into four cultural periods: the Aurignacian, the Gravettian, the Solutrean, and the Magdalenian. These subdivisions should not be taken too literally,

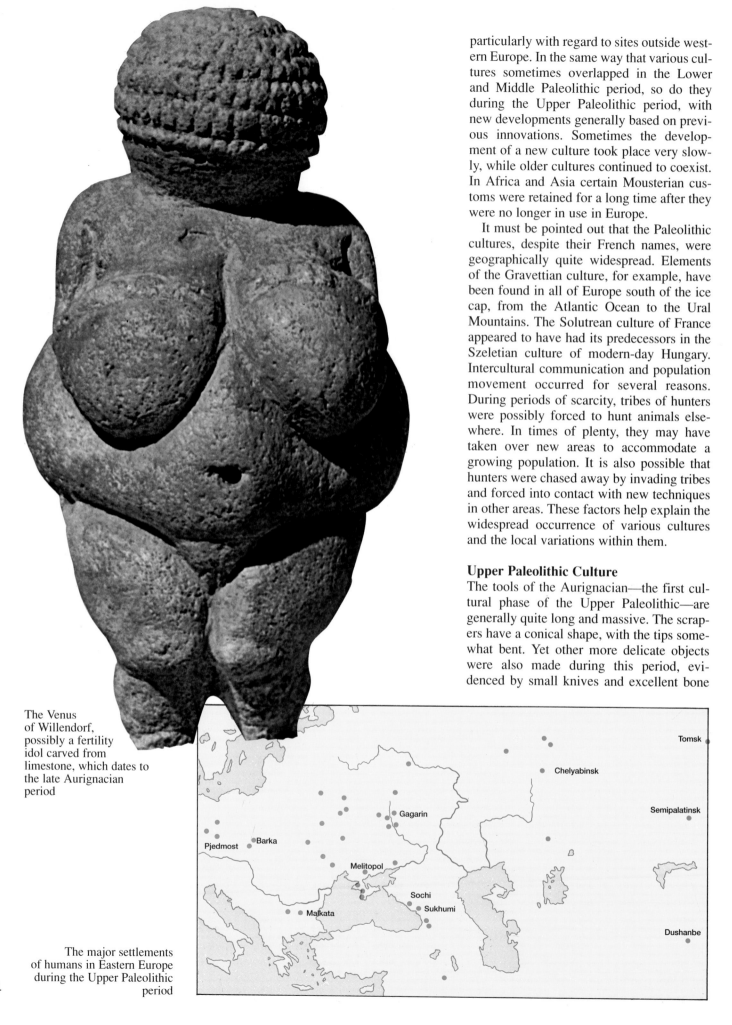

particularly with regard to sites outside western Europe. In the same way that various cultures sometimes overlapped in the Lower and Middle Paleolithic period, so do they during the Upper Paleolithic period, with new developments generally based on previous innovations. Sometimes the development of a new culture took place very slowly, while older cultures continued to coexist. In Africa and Asia certain Mousterian customs were retained for a long time after they were no longer in use in Europe.

It must be pointed out that the Paleolithic cultures, despite their French names, were geographically quite widespread. Elements of the Gravettian culture, for example, have been found in all of Europe south of the ice cap, from the Atlantic Ocean to the Ural Mountains. The Solutrean culture of France appeared to have had its predecessors in the Szeletian culture of modern-day Hungary. Intercultural communication and population movement occurred for several reasons. During periods of scarcity, tribes of hunters were possibly forced to hunt animals elsewhere. In times of plenty, they may have taken over new areas to accommodate a growing population. It is also possible that hunters were chased away by invading tribes and forced into contact with new techniques in other areas. These factors help explain the widespread occurrence of various cultures and the local variations within them.

Upper Paleolithic Culture

The tools of the Aurignacian—the first cultural phase of the Upper Paleolithic—are generally quite long and massive. The scrapers have a conical shape, with the tips somewhat bent. Yet other more delicate objects were also made during this period, evidenced by small knives and excellent bone

The Venus of Willendorf, possibly a fertility idol carved from limestone, which dates to the late Aurignacian period

Tomsk

Chelyabinsk

Semipalatinsk

Gagarin

Pjedmost   Barka

Melitopol

Sochi

Malkata   Sukhumi

Dushanbe

The major settlements of humans in Eastern Europe during the Upper Paleolithic period

Batons made of anther,
from the cave of Pendo,
with images of deer
and wild horses dating from
the Magdalenian period

points. The tools of the Gravettian period were characterized by knives made from blades and various types of bruins. No handles have been found.

The retouch on these instruments was, in general, quite rough in contrast to what is seen in the Solutrean tools. Most Solutrean lithics are long, narrow, and double-edged. They were flattened through a finishing process. Due to this flattened appearance, some of them are called "laurel leaves." Some objects look as if they might have been used as arrowheads, but no remains of bows and arrows have ever been found.

At the bottom of a gorge near Solutre, a mass grave of wild horses has been found. The horses were probably stampeded over the cliff by hunters using rocks and burning torches and then slaughtered. This technique, used in other cultures, including some native North American cultures, requires a high degree of organization and a considerable number of people in order to be successful.

The Magdalenian commenced toward the end of the Ice Age. Although Magdalenian culture has elements in common with the ones preceding it, it has enough entirely unique traits to be called a separate era. Traces of the Magdalenian have been found in all of western Europe, including certain areas of the North Sea that were dry at that time.

This hunting and gathering culture lasted from approximately 15,000 to 9,000 years before our era. During the Magdalenian peri-

Javelins made
of anther from the Magdalenian
period

55

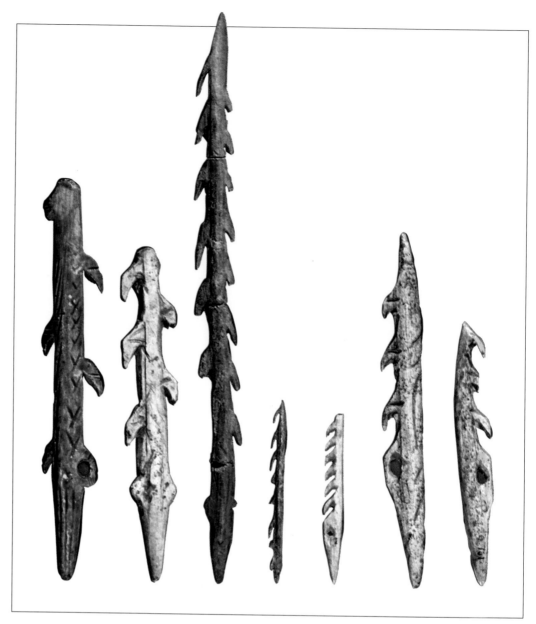

Harpoon carved
from bone, which dates to the
Magdalenian period

od, reindeer existed in great numbers in Europe. Mammoths were becoming extinct due to the increased warmth and wetness of the climate. This left the tundra open to the reindeer. The ice cap, during this period, came no farther than just south of Scandinavia. Magdalenian people spent much of their time hunting reindeer, depending on the animal as today's Laplanders still do. They used the hide for bedding and clothing, the meat for food, the tendons for sewing thread, and the bones and antlers for all sorts of tools. In the Magdalenian period, the use of flint decreased. The finer tools and functional objects were now nearly all made of bone or antler.

The first sewing needles have been found from this era. There is also evidence of great creativity in the making of spears. This skill reached a peak with the invention of the harpoon. As the climate improved and a new interglacial period dawned (in which we still live today), the tundra receded northward.

As this occurred, the reindeer disappeared and the western Magdalenian culture, so entwined with the great herds, drew to a close.

Artistic Expression

The beginning of the Upper Paleolithic period saw the appearance, for the first time in human evolution, of numerous representational objects and images that have generally been categorized under the term *Paleolithic art*. This is prior to the most famous cave paintings at Lascaux and Altamira, Spain (painted about 13,000 BC). However, the discovery of the painted caves of Chauvet (dated to 31,000 BC) in 1995 push the date back by nearly 15,000 years.

It is impossible to imagine that people with such a highly developed civilization did not also possess quite welldeveloped language skills. In this area, however, we find ourselves completely in the dark. Written language had not yet commenced. How

Modern interpretation depicting a person
from the Upper Paleolithic period
creating a wall paining

these people spoke will probably remain a
mystery. However, the people from these
great hunting cultures did leave behind illustrations of their daily activities. One of the
most surprising discoveries of the last century was that Ice Age people had highly developed artistic talent. Many prehistoric works
of art have been found in addition to the cave
paintings. It appears that symbolic expression began in the Paleolithic period.

Notable among the findings are carved
female figurines. Dozens of them in varied
form have been found. The figures are
thought to represent a sort of primordial
mother or fertility goddess. The fertility
aspect can certainly be assumed, since the
females depicted were usually pregnant and
their sexual characteristics quite clearly represented. These figurines are generally
thumb-sized and made of bone, ivory, or soft
stone. Some of them are a bit larger. In former Czechoslovakia, a very beautiful
expressive head has been found, with a hair-
net carved on it.

Findings from the Upper Paleolithic period also include animal figurines of stone,
ivory, and even baked clay. Most of these are
stylized carvings of mammoths or horses,
but some are lions, rhinoceroses, and bears.
Animal figures, deer and mountain goats,
have been found carved on the hand grips of
spearthrowers. Many of these are very clear,
anatomically accurate forms.

Thousands of Paleolithic engravings, dating from the Aurignacian era to the Magdalenian, have been found on cave walls, loose
stone plates, and objects made of bone. Most
of these were scratched into stone with a
stone tool. Some are done as reliefs, the
background cut away from the subject. They
depict a great variety of subjects, but once
again, animals predominate. Most common
are deer, bison, and lions, but fish and insects
have also been found and, occasionally, a
human face. Female figures are depicted,
rarely in groups. (Some pictures are quite

page 58-59

The left wall of the main
cavern of the caves
of Lascaux, France, with paintings
dating from the
Magdalenian period,
approximately 17,000 years ago

personal. In one image, a man looks, with nearly crossed eyes, at a naked woman.) Other pictures present information about hunting techniques, weapons, traps, and pitfalls. In the cave of La Colombière in France,

Head of a bull.
Painting in the caves
of Lascaux, France

excavated in 1913, the artists engraved sketches on bone and polished stones.

The Cave Paintings

Of all the artistic expressions from this prehistoric period, the cave paintings dating from 31,000 to 10,000 years ago are perhaps the most interesting. Particularly noteworthy are the multicolored paintings of Lascaux in France and Altamira in Spain, but some two hundred other caves in the south of France and Spain hold paintings. Most discoveries in this area are relatively new, and more are still being reported.

These cave paintings are mostly of animals, although some (especially the most recent) depict human figures. The animals are usually portrayed individually. Each animal is shown in profile (side view) with uninterrupted contours. Sometimes the animals are outlined with an engraved line. In other cases, the artist achieved a relief effect by making use of the irregularities of the stones to accentuate the body forms of the animals. Most of the paintings are done in a single color. Artists used various colors in only a few places, including Lascaux and Altamira. Colors were obtained from charcoal made from burned wood or bone, and ocher, mixed with vegetable juices, animal fats, egg white, or blood. Color nuances range from black, brown, and reddish to white. The artists painted with their fingers and used blowpipes to apply colors. Among the animals they illustrated, horses, mountain goats, deer, bison, mammoths, and reindeer predominated. Occasionally, they drew wolves, bulls, bears, lions, antelopes, wild boars, and, infrequently, birds and fish.

The paintings vary considerably in style and in content in accordance with the time they were made. The subject matter may have been a question of which animals the people wanted to kill or ward off. All of these paintings probably had a magical intent. Some Paleolithic cave paintings decorated the walls of rock chambers large enough to hold groups of ritual worshipers. Others were placed in passages less than a yard (meter) high where they could be seen only by torchlight. Some pictures were painted over with others, perhaps as part of some ritual.

These caves may have been considered holy places. No other evidence of permanent human occupation has been found in them, and it is quite possible they were used for the performance of magical rituals. This is indicated by a few paintings of human figures disguised as animals. The paintings may have been done to give power to the hunters or to predict the success of a hunt. Bison were frequently drawn, possibly to show how many of them there were and how vulnerable they were to the hunters. They were repeatedly depicted as under attack, sometimes with holes drawn to represent wounds in their bodies.

Although their purpose remains a matter of speculation, the paintings provide insight into the artistic abilities and the lifestyles of the ancient people who drew them.

Head of a stag. Painting in a cave near Alcoy, La Sarga, Alicante, Spain, dating from the Mesolithic period

The Mesolithic and Neolithic Periods

Hunters and Agricultural Civilizations

Tools made of stone and, to a lesser extent, bone and ivory, are evidence of human existence in the greatest part of the Paleolithic Age. A new period beginning around 10,500 BC is designated the Mesolithic. Also called the Middle Stone Age, the Mesolithic period is the ancient cultural stage that existed between the Paleolithic period and Neolithic period. While Paleolithic tools are made of chipped stone, and the Neolithic are of polished stone, Mesolithic tools are also made of chipped stone, and often they include very small stone tools that were mounted together on a shaft. These small tools are called

Stone arrowheads
from the Neolithic period,
found in the Sahara

microliths, and are often accompanied by a variety of bone, antler, and wooden tools, as well as some of polished stone.

Mesolithic usually points to a development that began about 8000 BC in northwestern Europe, after the end of the Pleistocene epoch. It lasted until about 2700 BC. Mesolithic cultures were known for adapting in many different ways to certain environments. Therefore the Mesolithic hunters were more successful than the hunters of the Paleolithic Age, utilizing many more vegetable and animal food

Stone axe from
the Mesolithic period,
c.9000 BC,
found in the Cau del Duc
near Gerona, Spain

sources. The changeover is based chiefly on the development, yet again, of new techniques in tool manufacture. A great many small artifacts have been found, dating from this time, that were fashioned with craftmanship similar to that of the Gravettians, but more refined.

In the 1930s, A. Rust defined a culture found in the vicinity of Hamburg, Germany, that showed great advance in tool manufacturing. One of the most significant finds here was a completely intact arrow. According to Rust, the find established that the arrow had already undergone a long period of development. The implication is that Paleolithic humans had made more technical progress than had been previously recognized. Of significance, as well, was the invention of the *atlatl*, or spear-thrower. This tool functioned as an extension of the human arm. It resembles a long wooden bat, grooved to hold the handle of a spear, with which the spear can be thrown with more force over a much greater distance than the individual can achieve. The hand grips of these tools were often particularly well made and artistically decorated.

Not much more than their tools has been recovered from the cultures of prehistoric

people. Nonetheless, important conclusions can be drawn, with caution, from these materials. A harpoon, for example, cannot be made without the knowledge of how to form its head and shaft and how to make and tie leather strips. A needle made of bone indicates that clothing, in that era, was made of pieces sewn together. This was confirmed by an important find of the Russian scholar O. Bader. In 1964 Bader found a grave in central Russia that held evidence of clothing about 25,000 years old. No actual clothing was ever recovered, but tools and adornments associated with clothes imply that it might have consisted of pants that could be fastened to shoes, some sort of jacket with a round neckline, and a hat. Decorations included beads made of mammoth ivory and reindeer teeth. The man, lying on a ceremonial bed of red ocher, had most likely been buried in his most beautiful clothing or in special burial clothes. Many types of tools and jewelry were buried with him, including a pair of ivory spears over seven feet (2.13 meters) long.

The Mesolithic Hunters

At the end of the last Ice Age the climate of the Northern Hemisphere changed. It became warmer and wetter and through the melting of the ice cap more lakes and oceans were created. The flora and fauna changed. The great herds of reindeer disappeared, or else moved north with the tundra. Humans adapted to the situation, exploiting the new

environment to their benefit. The Mesolithic era was an evolutionary challenge. Only a few groups of people followed the reindeer herds north with the ice. Most remained where they were, creating temporary camps in their familiar hunting areas and semipermanent seasonal camps elsewhere. There were evidently base camps for summer and winter. In them the gathering of edible plants and fruits increased significantly. Deer, boar, smaller game, and birds lived in the expanding forest cover and in the open fields and river deltas. Use of the bow and arrow for hunting increased. Seals, porpoises, and small whales were hunted with the aid of harpoons and canoes. Fishing increased in the rivers, lakes, and oceans with the use of bone hooks and harpoons.

Life during the Mesolithic Age is illustrated by a culture that existed in what is now Denmark. Signs of this culture have been found throughout the regions adjacent to the North Sea and the Black Sea. The people lived primarily from hunting. They had an extensive assortment of specialized tools made of bone, antlers, and stone. They hunted for moose, fox, and otter with the help of domesticated dogs. They fished with *leisters* (spears with barbed prongs), hooks, and harpoons. They used dugout canoes carved from tree trunks. (The oldest dugout canoe ever found is from this culture. Approximately 8,000 years old, it was discovered in the little town of Pesse in the Netherlands.) They established base camps in high dry

One aspect in which cave paintings from the Neolithic period differ from those of the Upper Paleolithic period is the active participation of people in the scenes represented. Bulls and hunters are depicted in this painting in the Cau del Moros, El Cogull, Lerida, Spain.

places near water and built wooden frame huts covered with straw. They probably outfitted them in accordance with the seasons. In the spring they fished for running salmon. In summer and autumn they gathered wild fruit and hazelnuts from the forests. They also collected eggs and the edible parts of water plants.

Much of what is known about this culture and others of that time can be credited to the peat bogs that existed at a few of the places they once inhabited. The bogs preserved otherwise perishable materials like wood and bone, neither of which rots under water.

While Mesolithic people generally lived in areas with mild climates, some groups of them moved on to the northern coast of Scandinavia. Here they probably made use of boats. Their traces have been found up to the White Sea in northeastern Russia. A Mesolithic culture was discovered in the Danish Ertebolle and named the *kjskkenmsddinger* or "kitchen waste middens" after its remains. This culture thrived along the North

Sea coasts, where its people gathered mussels and other mollusks. This type of food was so plentiful and so reliable a source that the people built permanent colonies there. In the same locale, they left behind enormous heaps of garbage, sometimes dozens of miles (50 kilometers) in circumference. These prehistoric refuse heaps have been found around the world. They first developed after the retreat of the glaciers and the disappearance of large Pleistocene animals that were hunted by prehistoric man. The oldest pottery of northern Europe, eastern North America and Central America has been found in these shell mounds.

Many shell mounds, especially on the eastern coast of Denmark, may have been used year-round, and contained the remains of four-legged animals, fish, birds, game, and mollusk shells that were all used for food. They also contained oysters, indicating that the shores where the oysters lived were open to the salt sea at the time. They were also used for human burial, although other more formal burial grounds existed. (The deceased were interred with burial gifts in both cases.) The kitchen midden culture existed during the late Mesolithic, spreading along the entire Atlantic coastline. Similar cultures are known from America (in a much later period), the coasts of the Caspian Sea, and the coasts of Australia.

Mesolithic people left other traces in the rest of Europe. South of the Pyrenees Mountains, which divide modern France and Spain, they painted hunting scenes on rock walls. They placed them near the openings to caves and on the back walls of the rock shelters under overhanging cliffs. Much more open to view than the work of their Paleolithic predecessors, the paintings lack the secretive character of the older work. In further contrast to the earlier cave paintings, these depict hunters and animals in motion. The people of this hunting culture of northern Spain, like those of other Mesolithic cultures, adopted Neolithic elements in their vessels and other containers, which were formed from clay and then fired at high temperature for durability.

Mesolithic cultures developed throughout the Near East. The most important of these was the Natufian, which spread along the entire eastern coast of the Mediterranean Sea. The Natufian was a Mesolithic culture of Palestine and southern Syria dating from about 9000 BC. They were mainly hunters, and also gatherers of wild grain. It is thought that they did not cultivate grain. They harvested the first mowing tools, sickles of flint blades set in straight bone handles. They also used stone mortars and pestles for grinding

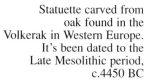

The canoe of Pesse, made from a pine tree, dating from the Mesolithic period, c.6000 BC

Statuette carved from oak found in the Volkerak in Western Europe. It's been dated to the Late Mesolithic period, c.4450 BC

Ivory female head, the Venus of Brassempouy, dating from the Aurignacian/Gravettian period, c.23,000 BC

the grain. Some Natufian groups lived in villages, while others lived in caves. They used cemeteries to bury their dead, and placed decorated personal items, including artwork of stone and bones with decorative carvings, in the burial places along with the bodies. Natufian people were hunters and fishermen. They also gathered large amounts of wild grain. This was remarkable, since grain must be processed in some way before consumption. The Natufian finds include the first mowing tools (sickles) and mortarlike grindstones. Nonetheless, these people were not farmers. Their harvest grew unattended, and there is no sign that they raised animals. (Domesticated animals can be differentiated from their wild counterparts by their smaller bones.) The collection of wild grain is a particularly labor-intensive task with an uncertain outcome. It is not surprising that these people began to think of ensuring a grain supply by growing their own near their living areas. The idea would completely change the world.

Neolithic Period

During the New Stone Age (Neolithic period), humans began to live in a completely

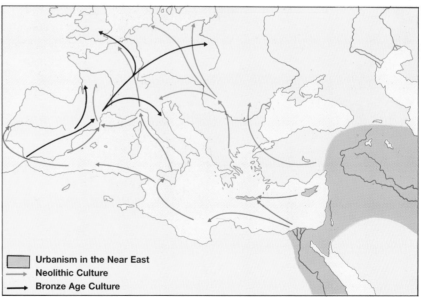

Urbanism in the Near East
Neolithic Culture
Bronze Age Culture

new way. From their first appearance until approximately 10,000 years ago, humans had been hunters and gatherers, living on the animals they scavenged or killed and the wild grains, berries, nuts, and other flora they collected. Although they did not stop hunting, they slowly became less dependent on animals for subsistence. Early humans

The Spread of Neolithic Culture in Europe

65

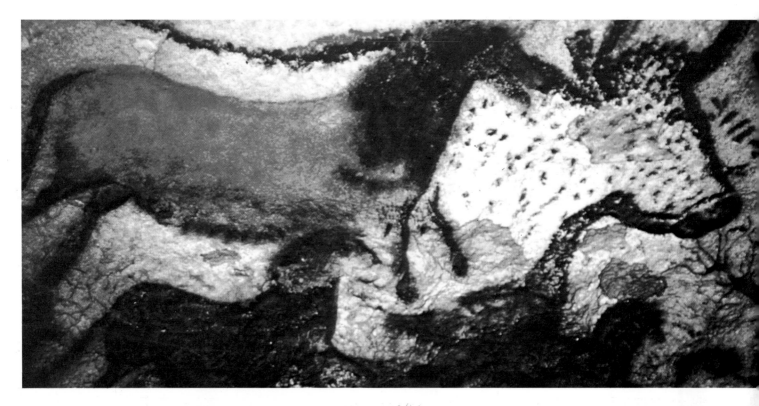

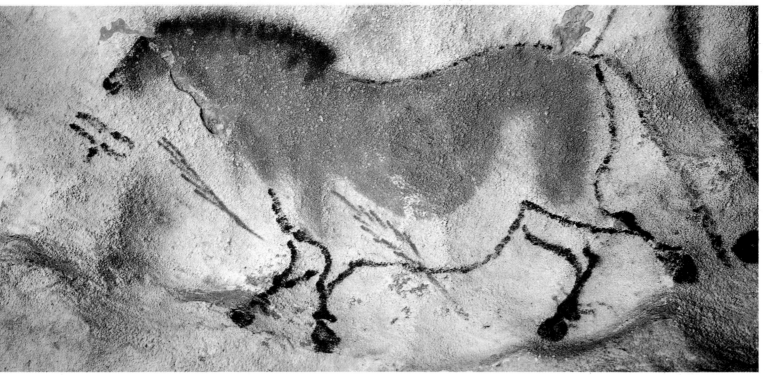

The Chinese Horse painting in the caves of Lascaux, France

had, as far as is known, also been gatherers of wild fruits, nuts, and other plants.

Most of what is known about them comes from archaeological finds of their tools, the materials they used, and the way they made them. The term *neolithic* itself is used to imply the change in new stone technology from chipped to polished stone. The changes that began 10,000 years ago were so great as to deserve the term *Neolithic revolution*.

The Neolithic revolution had to do with control of the production of food. The way in which humans sustained themselves was revolutionary in and of itself. Instead of hunting animals, humans turned to raising animals they could kill and eat at their convenience. Instead of foraging for plants, humans began to grow them, developing techniques of agriculture. This revolutionary production of food was a process that took place throughout the world. It had the same characteristics everywhere, regardless of continent. This agricultural revolution began in the valleys of the Tigris and Euphrates

Large bull accompanied
by a group of horses. Painting
in the caves of Lascaux, France

Rivers of Mesopotamia. It reached as far north as Scandinavia some 2,000 years before the present era. In other parts of the world, too, independent of the Near East, agricultural cultures appeared. In Central America people began to grow maize; in Asia, rice. Of course, there were groups of people who continued to practice their old ways. Certainly hunting continued. Still existing are less-developed cultures, such as the bushmen in Africa and the Aborigines in Australia, intact despite the onslaughts of the present century. (The parallel here is sociological, not individual. Individuals from those cultures are not limited to the immediate sociological perspectives that surround them. They can function entirely as equals in what is termed modern society, given adequate exposure and education.)

From a geographic viewpoint, the creative center of new development originated in southwest Asia in the area between the Mediterranean coast and the high plateau of Iran, and between the Persian Gulf and the Caucasus. It initiated the major changes of the Neolithic period. Evidently the peoples of southwestern Asia developed and applied new technologies of agriculture even earlier. In fact, the period preceding the Neolithic Age, the Mesolithic, already bore the first elements of cultural control of plants and animals.

The first attempts at the domestication of animals and plants apparently were made by peoples of the Mesolithic period. The tribes that hunted and gathered edible plants attempted to domesticate goats, dogs, and perhaps sheep as early as 9000 BC. But it was not until the Neolithic period that domestication was well under way. Dogs probably accompanied hunters and helped them in their hunting of wild animals. They may also have guarded settlements of people, warning the settlers of danger, as they do now. During the first stages of domestication, however, dogs were seen as food, and this was probably their main use.

The First Farmers
Originating in the Near East, the Neolithic lifestyle of agricultural civilization would extend over much of the Old World. The area around the Syrian Desert is called the "fertile

crescent." There, between the Taurus and Zagros Mountains and the inner reaches of the Levantine coast, was a great steppe area. Its annual rainfall allowed for the growth of huge amounts of grass with seeds that could be harvested. Neolithic people began to cultivate it, not simply harvest it. They domesticated grasses, which were to evolve into present-day grains. They used the oldest grains, spelt and barley, and wheat of the emmer, einkorn, and durum varieties. It is impossible to point to the precise place where agriculture was "discovered," but the place where Neolithic humans first lived has

been determined. The oldest traces of civilization in the Near East have been found.

Today the age of finds can be quite accurately determined with the aid of the C14 dating method, described earlier. It measures the radioactivity of certain carbon atoms. Since radiation in finds from the Paleolithic has weakened by now, this manner of dating cannot be as useful as it is for the Neolithic. Even here, since results can deviate by several centuries, it is rather unsuitable for dating the shorter historic periods within an entire era. (Dendrology, the dating method based on comparison of annual growth rings in trees, is more useful here. It can minimize the error.) These factors have significant bearing on the Neolithic settlements of Jericho and Abu Hureyra. Jericho, one of the best-known settlements of the Near East, lies in the valley of the Jordan River.

Here archaeologists have found ruins of the double-walled fortifications of the original Jericho established about 8000 BC by the Mesolithic Natufian culture. Above the

Polished stone
axes from the Neolithic
period

Natufian level are two layers revealing a number of characteristics of the then–new Neolithic lifestyle. Perhaps the oldest-known Neolithic settlement in the region is Abu Hureyra, situated on the Euphrates River in northern Syria. Neolithic characteristics evident in both settlements are permanent dwellings and large grinding stones for processing grain.

Archaeological evidence shows that the cultures at the beginning of the Neolithic in the Near East did not yet use earthenware. The age of pottery-making had not yet dawned. The first earthenware excavated in Jericho was found in its most recent layers. Significantly, what was found in the oldest layers were bones of domesticated goats. The new farmers had apparently learned quite rapidly to adapt themselves to life in permanent settlements. Between the grain they grew and the livestock they raised, they were no longer entirely dependent on what nature provided. They began to manipulate their environment for survival.

Agriculture and Property

Jericho is on the west side of the Jordan Valley. It is one of the world's earliest continuous settlements, dating perhaps from about 9000 BC. Jericho is famous in biblical history as the first town attacked by the Israelites under Joshua after they crossed the Jordan. Jericho is mentioned often in the Old and New Testaments. Herod the Great established a winter residence there, and that is where he died in 4 BC. The Roman and New Testament city of Jericho is located about one mile (1.6 kilometers) south of the location of the Old Testament city.

Excavations have shown that Jericho had a very long history before the biblical period, and the site's great importance is that it provides evidence of the first development of permanent settlements and therefore signs of the first movement toward civilization.

The size of the walled settlement that was discovered is what justifies the use of the term *town* and suggests a population at the time of from 2,000 to 3,000 persons. In the course of 1,000 years there had been an evolution to settlement from a hunting way

Flint knives and scrapers from the Neolithic period

Hand grindstones from the late Neolithic period, found in the Levant (Israel, Palestine, Jordan)

of life. This is where the development of agriculture comes in, since grains of cultivated wheat and barley have been found there, and there is the possibility that irrigation was invented there.

The first pottery-users of Jericho were primitive compared with those who had occupied the site before them. They were pastoral and lived in simple huts sunk in the ground. An urban culture once more appeared in Jericho at the end of the fourth millenium BC, as it did in the rest of Palestine. This is when Jericho became a

walled town again. The Canaanites introduced town life to Jericho later, and evidence of their domestic furniture has been found. The furniture was located in tombs, where it was placed to be used by the dead in the afterlife. The Israelites adopted much of this Canaanite culture.

The Jericho of Herod was revealed in 1950–1951, when excavations uncovered an exceptional facade a mile (1.6 kilometers) south of Old Testament Jericho. It was probably part of Herod's palace, and its Italian style is an example of Herod's devotion to Rome. This building was the center of Roman Jericho.

A mile (1.6 kilometers) east of the Old Testament site was yet a third discovery, Jericho of the Crusader period. It was here that the modern town was born.

The oldest Jericho had the character of a permanent settlement, with houses made of sun-hardened clay tiles and heavy surrounding walls and towers. This points to the fact that the residents of Jericho had to protect themselves from enemy attack. In the earlier hunting cultures, the members of various tribes vied for control of hunting grounds, in some sense reflecting a concept of property. The new agriculturists, however, took definite possession of certain areas at the expense of nomadic tribes.

The initial contact between farmers and pastoralists (or hunters and gatherers) was probably not hostile, although there may have been occasional disputes. In any case, the first farmers did not seem to require the sturdy enclosing walls of the later Jericho.

Some of the earliest remaining examples of mudbrick house construction. These structures date to the Neolithic period of Catal Hüyük, Turkey.

The second Neolithic layer bears the marks of a different culture. Here, round houses were replaced by square ones, and the burial customs changed. In the oldest Jericho culture, the heads of the deceased were placed separate from the bodies in circles or "nests." In the second culture, the flesh was removed from the heads. They were layered with plaster, which was then sculpted to the shape of the face and painted.

This second group of Jericho inhabitants failed to survive. For several thousand years, the city was populated by successive groups of people. Time and time again, new cultures moved in on top of the piles of waste and ruins of the old. Each successive wave formed a new "living layer" above the old. Eventually, a hill was built up, dozens of feet high, called a "tell." Such tells occur quite frequently in the Near East. Each strategic layer of an excavation contains the clues to interpret the society that formed it.

Jarmo, also called Qalat Jarmo, is a prehistoric archaeological site located east of Kirkuk, in present-day Iraq, an area that was first occupied around 7000 BC. The site is important because it revealed traces of what was one of the world's first village-farming communities. Jarmo yielded twelve layers of history. There is evidence of domesticated barley and wheat, of goats and dogs, all of which suggests a settled agricultural way of life.

The settlement called Jarmo flourished in Kurdistan, in northern Mesopotamia, approximately 6,000 years ago. The village consisted of round huts made of braided fiber covered with clay. As expected, there is evidence of the processing of obsidian (volcanic glass), common at the time in that region. The earthenware found in Jarmo, however, was unique. It represents the first known use of such pottery technique. Jarmo agriculture also proved to have developed further than that of early Jericho. Leftover bones revealed that the amount of game used for food decreased in comparison with that of domesticated animals.

Trade and Animal Husbandry

A third Neolithic center is evident in southern Turkey, indicating the diffusion of agriculture toward Europe. Eleven cultural

Ceramic technology was one of the major technological innovations which emerged during the Neolithic period. Neolithic pot from southern Spain

Female figurine
from the Neolithic period,
possibly representing fertility
and abundance.
Found at Catal Hüyük
in Turkey.

layers, one on top of the other, have been excavated in Catal Hüyük, dating from 7000 to 5000 BC. This settlement, like Jericho, had an urban character. Its houses were built together in a large block. The interior walls were decorated with paintings and reliefs, usually figures of animals and geometric patterns. Some depict what may be a fertility

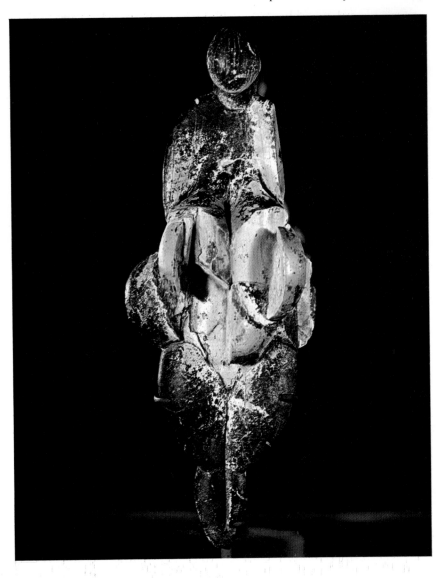

Small female figure, the Venus of Lespugue, carved from the ivory of a mammoth. This figure dates to the Upper Paleolithic.

from the roof level, presumably via a wooden ladder. The houses had platforms for working, sitting, and sleeping. They also had ovens and hearths.

It has been found that edible grains and nuts and seeds that produced oil were cultivated here. Animal husbandry was practiced as well. The religious shrines unearthed here are known for the brilliance of their wall paintings, which are a link to the Upper Paleolithic art.

The city at Catal Hüyük appears to have been a center of trade in obsidian. This is consistent with the rise of trade typical of the Neolithic period. Agriculture offered such a degree of food production that some farmers could begin to concern themselves with trade or crafts.

An equally old settlement was Cayönu in Turkey. An extensive range of Neolithic agricultural instruments has been found here, including scythes and millstones. The oldest vessels known, made of hollowed-out stones, also come from this site.

The cultural range of the Fertile Crescent continued to expand. Contact with other people and the mutual exchange of concepts and techniques increased. This was evident, as well, in the development of animal husbandry and the use of various species of animal. Sheep and goat had been indigenous to this area. There were domestic cattle in 7000 BC in Egypt, and pigs appear to have been first domesticated around the same time in the region of modern-day Turkey and Greece. (The dog, not bred for meat, had already been domesticated much earlier, probably as early as 12,000 BC in Europe.)

For certain cultural groups in regions unsuitable for agriculture, the keeping of animals became the primary means of subsistence. Such societies developed later than those linked to agriculture. (The cattle-based culture of the Masai in northeast Africa is a modern-day example.) Societies based on animal husbandry were generally nomadic, following the herds they depended on, like the reindeer hunters of the Upper Paleolithic Age. (They even attempted some taming of the reindeer.) A difficulty in the anthropologic study of these nomadic cultures is the fact that, by their very nature, they left few traces behind.

goddess of agriculture and a bull-worshiping cult. Bulls figured prominently in a form of religion found later throughout the entire Mediterranean area.

Catal Hüyük (sometimes written as one word) is a major Neolithic site in the Middle East, located in Konya province, Turkey. The surrounding plain was probably a natural choice for a stock-breeding and agricultural settlement. The excavations that took place in 1961 and a few years thereafter showed this to be the center of an advanced culture. The earliest period of building ascribed to this site tentatively dates to about 6700 BC, and the latest to about 5650 BC. The inhabitants lived in rectangular mud-brick houses. They probably entered them

The Neolithic Period

The Spread of Agriculture

Neolithic culture spread from the Fertile Crescent, which includes areas in present-day Iraq, Iran, Syria, Jordan, Turkey, and Israel, to southern Russia, India, and North Africa. This new civilization exhibited a sedentary way of life in comparison with the past. The powerful societies of the Nile Valley and Mesopotamia would develop from it a few thousand years later. The most rapid advance of Neolithic culture, however, was to Europe, by way of the land bridge of Turkey and the Balkan Peninsula. The oldest settlements in the north of Greece appeared shortly after 7000 BC and show evidence of Turkish influence. The Straits of Bosporus and the Dardanelles apparently presented no obstacles, nor did the Aegean Sea between Greece and the island of Crete. The earliest influences of Neolithic Greek culture began to appear on Crete. There is evidence that the islands of Cyprus and Mallorca were also inhabited by Neolithic peoples. It is likely

Bandkeramik found in a settlement of the culture named after this kind of pottery near Vaux-en-Borset, Belgium, c.4000 BC

Black bison.
Painting in the caves
of Lascaux, France

that some degree of contact and exchange existed among them.

By 5000 BC, the new culture had already reached well into Europe. The Italian Peninsula, the island of Sicily, and the Mediterranean coasts of France and Spain showed its influence. The extensive changes in climate and topography after the Ice Age slowly brought a Neolithic lifestyle to many different groups of people throughout the world. The new use of agriculture spread north to the Caucasus Mountains between the Black Sea and the Caspian in southern Russia and moved east to Turkistan and Afghanistan. Via the Persian Gulf to the southeast, it neared the valley of the Indus River of the Indian subcontinent. Most of the Nile Valley was familiar with agriculture by then. (Egyptian agriculture is probably an indigenous development.)

Around 4000 BC Neolithic culture extended to the Sudan and along the coast of North Africa to Morocco. In western Europe, the rest of Spain, France, and England were affected. Only northern Scotland and Scandinavia now lay outside the range of the new civilization, probably due to their colder climate.

Large portions of Asia and all of the American continents appear to have remained outside the reach of this Neolithic diffusion. A similar pattern of growth from hunting to agriculture would subsequently occur in both regions.

Extensive agricultural civilizations would arise in China. It is virtually certain that they were of independent origin. Previous schools of archaeology considered the Neolithic civilizations of China to have originated earlier than those of the Middle East. Today the Middle East is regarded as the earliest. Southeast Asia must be viewed as the origin of various cultures, defined by the fruit or the grain in predominant use (mango, breadfruit, banana, and probably also rice). In that region, as well, the first poultry and certain other animals were domesticated. An independent Neolithic civilization may have arisen in the fertile areas between Malaysia and Burma.

The origin of Neolithic culture on the American continents is more certain. Prehistoric cultural remains in the Americas are completely separate from those of the Old World. There is no direct relationship between the Neolithic of the Old World and that of the New World. Although animal husbandry began quite late in Central America, agriculture developed early, giving rise to the great Mayan and Aztec civilizations. Tomatoes, cocoa, potatoes, and maize were grown. The Incas would flourish in Peru, domesticating the llama.

The Earthenware Trail West
The diffusion of Neolithic culture can be fol-

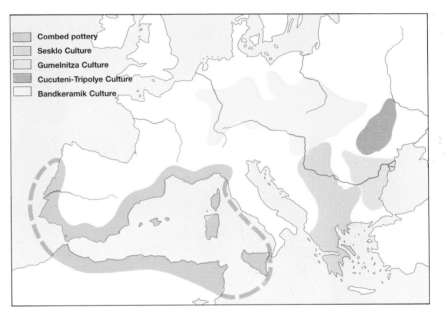

Areas of Distribution
of the First European Cultures
Characterized by
Specific Pottery

lowed by means of the earthenware remains left by its varied peoples. The spread should be viewed as the work of small-scale societies, which over and over again developed far-ranging trading networks and established settlements at distant points. This intensive migration is a feature associated with the nature of Neolithic agriculture.

From northern Greece, the trail led to cultural centers in the Balkans, like Starcero in the region of southern Slavia, which blossomed as early as 5000 BC. Localized branches appeared in Bulgaria and Hungary, the valley of the Danube, and along an extension of the Rhine into the Netherlands. In the more northernly areas of Europe, the important culture of *linear bandkeramik* developed, named after the earthenware it pro-

Idol from the
Neolithic period of Eastern Europe,
carved from bone and
incised with geometric lines, Tell
Metchkur, Bulgaria

duced. This earthenware had a characteristic decorative pattern of wavy or zigzag lines. The bandkeramik potters extended their culture through the valleys of the Rhine, the Dniester, the Weichsel, and the Elbe. The culture spread over an extensive area, con-

Head of a Neolithic statuette found in Tell Karcheff, Bulgaria

secutively reaching Poland, Germany, Switzerland, France, Belgium, and the Netherlands, while branching off to Russia and the Baltic coasts.

Migrating Farmers

The Rhine, the Dniester, the Weichsel, and the Elbe were the connecting roads of the Neolithic culture in Europe, the avenues of the long period of slow migration associated generally with the nature of New Stone Age agriculture. The surplus food supplies contributed to a condition that could support an unparalleled population explosion, one that time and time again resulted in the migration of groups or families. As they relocated, they brought along their own lifestyles, learning from and influencing the people already there. The end result was a high degree of cultural variety and development.

Because no concepts of fertilization or crop rotation were known, these Neolithic farmers repeatedly planted crops on the same plots of land. This resulted in depletion of the soil. It is no coincidence that agricultural civilizations in Egypt and Mesopotamia, where flooding kept the fields fertile, reached the highest level. The farmers continually sought new agricultural land, often burning off a section of forest to plant. (This is termed slash-and-burn agriculture.) Sometimes, years after leaving a place, they would return to an area only to find it occupied by other people. This led variously to battle or compromise and intercultural exchange.

As far back as 5000 BC, bandkeramik farmers reached the Low Countries on the North Sea. Dozens of their settlements have been found in the Netherlands and the Belgian Limburg. Originally they came from Germany, where nearly identical settlements have been found in the region of Cologne. They showed a marked preference for loessial soil (a fine-grained, yellowish brown loam usually deposited by the wind) because of its fertility. Areas where it was found were high and dry enough for agriculture. They scratched the ground open with sticks or stone axes, breaking up large clumps of earth with rocks. They grew barley and three types of wheat (emmer, einkorn, and durum). They raised cattle, sheep, goats, and pigs as domestic animals inside fenced-off areas and occasionally led the herds through the river valleys. Evidence of bones indicates that they also hunted game. They had only sporadic contact with the people still adhering to Mesolithic ways who lived much lower down in the valleys. Agriculture and animal husbandry made it possible to have larger families and larger tribes. Some bandkeramik villages comprised dozens of houses, and villages were often located near each other. The older hunters and gatherers required significantly more space, even for quite small groups. The farming tribes quickly overcame their old-fashioned neighbors in both number and strength.

Archaeological Clues

No ruins of bandkeramik residences remain.

Their houses were built of temporary materials like wood and bark. Nonetheless, they did leave traces behind. Archaeologists have searched for such traces as clues to their culture. Underlying the search was the fact that ground will always bear the traces of anything that has disturbed it. For example, an abandoned ditch will eventually fill up with soil and dead leaves. This humuslike substance will show up as darker than the surrounding ground. Similarly, poles set in the ground will disintegrate over a period of time but leave visible discoloration where they were.

Tells, or artificial hills made of layers of soil over ancient ruins, can offer evidence to archaeologists. Tells appear when mud brick has been used in building over time (shortages of fuel made mass production of brick impossible). These structures were highly vulnerable to the elements and had to be constantly renewed, generation after generation. Layers of settlement accumulated, creating a mound of debris marking the site of habitation, the mound being known as a tell. They are found after centuries of human dwelling on the same spot.

The sites of the ancient cities of Troy and Ur are examples of tells. Ur, known also as Tell El Mugayyar, was an important city of ancient southern Mesopotamia (Sumer) situated about 140 miles (225 kilometers) southeast of the site of Babylon, and founded sometime in the fourth millennium BC. Its settlers were thought to have been farmers. In antiquity the river ran closer to the city, and it was the change in the river's course that left the ruins in a desert that was once fertile land. Every stage in the city's many lives had been illustrated.

The discovery of Ur is typical of the tell (also *tall* or *tel*; in Turkish *tepes* or *huyuks*), a characteristic form of Mesopotamian ruin. *Tell*, and many forms of the word, is a term found among the earliest Semitic languages as early as the end of the third millennium BC.

The tell's characteristic mound formation makes excavation particularly difficult, since both the vertical and horizontal have to be carefully unearthed and examined. The depths of various levels are not constant.

The excavation of a bandkeramik settlement in Sittard (in the Netherlands) revealed, in a single carefully leveled layer, no less than forty-four farms. The farms were mapped out by large spots, where poles had once been driven, and dark strips, where walls once stood. Ditches were found in adjacent peat bogs where the peat moss had been taken out to cover the walls. They were later used as sites for waste disposal. Most of the houses proved to have been over 30

Neolithic idol carved from bone with incised markings, found in Moron de la Frontera, Spain

Small flint knife found in San Vicente de Castellet, Spain

yards (27.43 meters) long and approximately 7 yards (6.4 meters) wide. The northwest sides of the buildings, judging from their more solid construction, apparently served as living quarters. The remaining sides formed sheds or stalls. Large amounts of flint waste were found in one of the houses. Someone had obviously processed stones there.

Careful ground study can sometimes yield more information about old cultures than excavated objects, as long as the ground has not been disturbed. Plant remains or pollen grains sometimes play a very important role in this. Pollen grains are resistant to all kinds of outside influences and they survive for thousands of years. Every type of plant has a typical shape recognizable under a microscope. From this information, the plant growth of an area at a particular time can be established. This method is called pollen analysis. (It is essential that the pollen sample be taken from an undisturbed area such as a lake bed or a peat bog.) It makes it possible to reconstruct the environment in a given location. showing what the landscape looked like, what was grown in the area, and what influence people had. For example, the pollen count from the elm tree of a bandkeramik excavation decreases in the higher layers (a phenomenon called elm drop). This could quite possibly mean that the number of elms in that region decreased because people cut down the trees to use the leaves and twigs as winter feed for their domesticated animals.

The significance of the pollen method does not deny the importance of Neolithic object finds. Apart from earthenware and tools made of flint, objects made of other kinds of stone have been discovered. These are characteristic of the New Stone Age. They include chisels and adzes for woodworking, sharpening stones, and grindstones. What is remarkable is that most of these tools were made of nonindigenous types of rock, stones that did not occur locally. Probably they were imported as finished or semimanufactured tools from the Rhine area.

Studies of earthenware are of great significance in the study of prehistoric times. Certain earthenware finds indicate that the bandkeramik potters must have had contact with tribal relatives in the east. Although the oldest Neolithic civilizations probably did not yet produce earthenware, a culture is usually considered no longer Mesolithic when ceramic pottery is found. The new lifestyle created new demands in methods of storage. The old tools were inadequate for storing milk and flour. Baskets covered with clay, leather pouches, and hollowed-out gourds were used less frequently in settled groups. The early potters simply reproduced such objects in clay, but because clay was so easy to shape, a variety of models was soon made to accommodate new needs.

Neolithic ceramic vessel incised decoration. The decoration is probably symbolic.

Tradition and Change

As in earlier times, people continued to be bound by tradition. Typically, once a culture has established a certain form and pattern of decoration, it is maintained for many years. Changes, unless they are the result of outside influence from other groups, generally occur quite slowly. For this reason, cultures can be identified even by very small shards (broken pieces) of pottery. They provide a reliable guide in the archaeological world.

After the bandkeramik people, other cultures appeared with other types of pottery. Neolithic influence continued to spread from the Mediterranean region to the rest of Europe. By about 3500 BC it extended to England, Spain, northern Italy, Switzerland, and France in many different cultures with separate characteristics. All of these, however, had certain commonalities. In each, people continued to maintain some Mesolithic practices, often living from hunting and gathering, in addition to agriculture and animal husbandry. They frequently mixed easily with the older Mesolithic tribes.

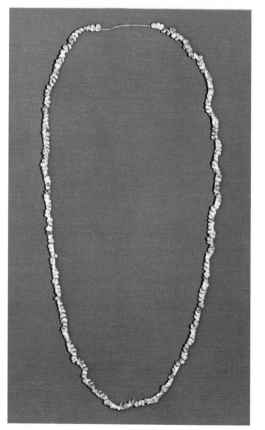

Neolithic necklace consisting of a string of snail shells

Large stone constructions, graves and temples, are typical of the end of the Neolithic period. Dolmen (stone table),
a burial chamber built with large stone slabs and covered by a flat stone, in Vallgorguin Barcelona, Spain

Prehistoric Humans

Miners, Farmers, and Tradesmen

The archaeological world was excited to discover that mining practices had existed as far back as prehistoric times. Ancient humans liked to make their tools from two materials, flint and obsidian, a black volcanic glass. These two materials are easy to shape and as hard as glass, but they are relatively hard to locate. Early mining involved locating flint, the most important material of the Stone Age. Found in calcium-rich areas, flint is a very hard stone, a kind of quartz that occurs in horizontal layers in Cretaceous (or chalk) formations. Such layers of flint also exist on the surface of Earth. Some of these layers were sources of the stone as early as the Middle Paleolithic period. They offered a far more efficient means of supply than the random search for isolated outcroppings of the stone.

On the European continent various Neolithic people began applying their technical skills to the mining of flint, which could then be traded for food. These mining activities lasted for nearly 2,000 years. They

Entrance to the Balzal Rossi in Liguria, Italy, where implements from the Neolithic period were found. Although people had started to settle in small village communities by then, the caves were still used as burial places.

began around 4000 BC and took place in what is today France, Germany, England, and later in the areas that are today Scandinavia and Poland. The mines in Spiennes (Belgium) have yielded the most evidence concerning early mining technology.

The Prehistoric Flint Industry

After the early miners had exhausted the resources of the upper surface layers, they hacked out vertical shafts, sometimes up to 50 feet (15.24 meters) deep. When they came to a layer of flint, they constructed horizontal tunnels radiating from that point outward. *Bandkeramik* (earthenware) makers and their successors, including the Rössen and the Michelsberg cultures, practiced mining. They used pickaxes, which were made of deer antler or flint, outfitted with wooden handles. Flint deposits are found in chalk formations. The miners brought the chunks of flint they found to the surface and dumped the useless chalk into abandoned mine tunnels. They occasionally used strong sapling poles to provide support in the mine shafts, but cave-ins did occur. In the mine at Obourg, the skeleton of a prehistoric miner has been found buried, with his pickax in hand, under a cave-in. Industrial accidents must have occurred quite often. The miners did their work in tunnels less than three feet high (under one meter), with minimal lighting. All of this would have taken place amid clouds of dust and gravel. The flint was roughly processed, hewn into usable chunks in workshops near the mine, and traded in that unfinished condition. Its buyers could further shape the semimanufactured material to their own needs. Rough hunks of flint like this have been found over a large part of Europe.

The earthenware products from mining areas were often characterized by such objects as the "tulip beaker" pottery typical of the Michelsberg culture. Evidence of this culture has been found throughout the area between Bohemia and the Netherlands.

The Funnel-Beaker Culture

Around 2500 BC, large parts of Europe came under the influence of a new culture, called Funnel-beaker after the characteristic conical shape of its earthenware. Its people shared ceramic types but probably did not otherwise share a cohesive culture, as they were spread over a large range that lay north of the early Michelsberg cultural area, eastward into Poland, and northward to Denmark and southern Sweden. While the cosmology and the social organization of these people varied, the Funnel-beaker culture as a whole was built on a Mesolithic foundation, as is evidenced by its tools made of flint. However, its people had adopted agriculture on the Neolithic model. They grew barley and wheat, raised livestock (cows, sheep, goats, and pigs) and, less intensively, hunted (beaver, otter, red deer, roe, or wild boar) and fished (pike and bass). The farmers of the Funnel-beaker culture grew their crops on relatively small plots of land prepared by burning down wooded areas. When they depleted the soil in one area, they prepared another plot beside it and left the first one as meadowland. These farmers also appear to have usually kept their animals penned inside fenced areas and to have used elm leaves as animal feed.

The buildings of the Funnel-beaker people are well known from excavations in Denmark and Germany. In Jutland (Denmark), a structure built entirely on heavy beams driven into the ground has been discovered. It is over 250 feet (76 meters) long and has no less than twenty-six rooms. These were intended to accommodate several families. In Oldenburg, a village has been found that contained forty houses. Each measured approximately 13 by 16 or 16 by 22 feet (3.7 x 4.8 or 4.8 x 6.7 meters). All of them had two rooms and a porch. The walls were made of woven fibers, plastered with clay. The floors were made of tree trunks.

While local variations no doubt existed, given their vast cultural expanse, universal characteristics of the social structure of the Funnel-beaker people have been established. Their settlements were typically located

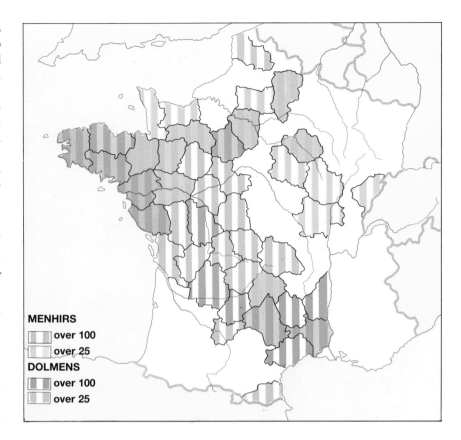

MENHIRS
over 100
over 25
DOLMENS
over 100
over 25

Spread of the
Megalithic Monuments
in France

Menhirs are the
religious monuments from
the Megalithic cultures
of the Late Neolithic period.
Although mostly found
in Brittany, they also occur
elsewhere in Europe,
such as this menhir
in Romanya de la Selva,
Gerona, Spain.

81

Menhirs placed in rows, known as alignments, near Carnac, Morbihan, France

adjacent to areas rich in peat. Peat bogs can preserve objects quite well, adding a tanning effect due to the fact that the water itself acts as a preservative. Sealed off from air, many objects were preserved in the peat bogs that would otherwise have dissolved in ordinary soil. Some of these were apparently deposited in the peat on purpose, perhaps as offerings. Among the items retrieved are picks made of bone, tool handles, bowls, and paddles made of wood. There is even a sacrificial pot of food containing a fine meal of egg with fish and two types of meat.

The name of this culture comes from the typical conical shape of its pottery. The people also made what are termed *collared bottles*, spherical bottles with a protruding edge at the top, suitable for fastening to a carrying cord. In addition to pots, pitchers, bowls, and platters, "baking sheets" have been found, large tiles of fired clay used to hold food for baking. All of these forms showed a certain similarity in style and decorative pattern. The clay was decorated by the use of a wooden or bone spatula before it was fired. Another decorative effect was created by the use of a stick wrapped with thread. Some earthenware findings point to extensive

intercultural contact and the existence of specialists in the craft of pottery.

Many ceramic findings have been unearthed from the megaliths (or megalithic burial monuments, in archaeological terms) built by the Funnel-beakers. The most plentiful discoveries of visible monuments dating from the second to the fourth millenium are chamber tombs, which were sometimes cut out of rock. More commonly, though, they were built from the megalithic blocks that were surrounded by smaller stones that were packed into place by overlying mounds.

These were burial places for successive generations of clans or families, and their construction involved social and physical advancement comparable to the building of churches in early historic times. There is religious feeling evident here, as well, and great

Burial chambers built from large erratic blocks, found in Western Europe

83

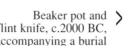
Beaker pot and
flint knife, c.2000 BC,
found accompanying a burial
at Barnwood

Passage grave
from the Megalithic culture
in Apulia, Italy

attention has been paid to the symbolic designs that have been carved, painted, or pecked on the stones used to build these megalithic structures.

The Funnel-beakers exhibited great technical abilities, evident in the peat bridges they built. Made of parallel tree trunks, these formed a road across otherwise inaccessible swamps. They undoubtedly served cart traffic. At one such bridge, a wooden wagon wheel has been recovered.

Vläardingen Culture

A number of settlements at the periphery of the Funnel-beaker lands are attributed to the Vläardingen culture. This is named after a site in the Netherlands where findings date back over 2,000 years. The people of this culture continued hunting and fishing in the river deltas as they took up agriculture and animal husbandry. They hunted deer, wild boar, otter, and beaver. They fished for sturgeon and other river fish using knotted nets and wicker fykes (long bag nets kept open by a series of hoops).

They had vehicles of transport and large houses (32 by 18 feet or 9.7 x 5.4 meters). Around these houses they grew small crops of grain and raised livestock. (At a later point they raised larger livestock in inland grassy meadows.) They collected mussels at settlements along the northern North Sea coast.

Neolithic
double pot with
geometrical
decoration

Earthenware
bell-beakers from the
beginning of the
second millennium BC
were found over a
large area of Europe.
This is an early bell-beaker
from Ciempozuelos,
Spain.

The Vläardingen culture was quite flexible, its people able to do many things. They had elaborated on their Mesolithic technology using Neolithic techniques including pottery making. Nonetheless, their work exhibits some unity of design. The people of the Vläardingen culture knew at least twelve different objects and models, including the baking sheet. Since there were no suitable stones in the coastal areas where they lived, they had to import mill and hammer stones from the Ardenne area (in present-day Belgium) and axes from the mining areas of Germany. How they obtained such objects and how they "paid" for them remains a mystery. Evidently the imported tools were valuable, as they made the broken ones into scrapers and pointed tools called burins. They made tools of deer antler and bone, as well. Vläardingen settlements have also been found further inland, all situated on coastal embankments. There were probably quite a few other sites along the principal rivers.

Herdspeople from Southern Russia

At around 2200 BC northern Europe was invaded by a type of herdspeople who were bearers of the "Single-grave culture." This culture was named after a form of ceramic.

These people had been driven out of their original living areas in the southern Russian steppes either by other groups of people or by drought. They successfully relocated themselves farther westward. Because the central European plateau at that time was still mostly covered with forest, the herdspeople first had to burn down large areas of forest to prepare grazing pasture. They stayed for some time, using that ground, but then continued west, searching for new land. Since this ground was likely to have been occupied, it is assumed that they were a warlike people who did not hesitate to usurp the land from its previous inhabitants. This characterization is supported by the most ubiquitous tool of the people, known as the battle-ax.

It is not entirely understood whether or not these were actually battle-axes. In many of them, the opening for the handle is so narrow that it could not possibly have been used to deal hard blows. The actual battle-ax may have been a type of small ax with an extra long, blunt end.

The ceramics of these people is characterized by a high concentration of cups with molded bases and horizontally placed decorations. Unfortunately, we only know them

Tumuli and Megaliths

Burial customs and burial monuments play a great role in archaeology. They are often the only evidence of past cultures. The attention given to the dead provides insight into the thinking of the people who buried them.

Tumuli (mounds) is the Latin word given to the burial mounds of the Neolithic cultures of the Funnel-beaker and Protruding-foot beaker people. The deceased was laid to rest in a field or a shallow hole in the ground. He or she was usually placed in a sleeping position, lying on a side, with one arm up toward the head and the knees drawn up. A mound of earth, demarcated by circles of poles, circular trenches, or stone monuments, was piled over the body. Often little more remains of the skeleton than a light discoloration in the ground, called the corpse silhouette.

The burial gifts, items buried in the mounds with the dead, offer considerable information about prehistoric man. Death was apparently regarded as a transition into further life, with the person who died evidently still expected to require a variety of things to do with daily existence. These were buried with the body and included tools, weapons, stones, and, later, bronze pots and pans filled with food and drink.

The *tumuli* varied in size, ranging from small elevations in the landscape to large hills. Ordinary flat graves and evidence of cremation have been noted within the same culture as burial mounds.

Prehistoric stone monuments have been found throughout Europe, the oldest dating from around 4000 BC. The largest of these are called megaliths, from the Greek *mega* (large) and *lith* (stone). It is not clear why such monuments were built. There are indications that their construction may have been a local phenomenon, but they also show some influence from the eastern Mediterranean region.

The people of the Funnel-beaker culture made large *tumuli*, demarcated by *dolms* (circles of megaliths). They used these as communal graves, where they buried their dead, generation after generation.

Megalithism, the building of monuments of large stones, can be differentiated into three main categories. *Alignments*, noted mainly in Brittany, are long rows of monuments. The most well known are those in the

Carnac area, presumed to have some function associated with sun cults.

Individually placed megaliths, found all over Europe, are called *menhirs* (from the Breton *men*, meaning stone, and *hir*, long). They may or may not have been associated with a megalithic grave. Menhirs were erected most frequently in western Europe and were often found placed together to form circles, semicircles, or massive ellipses. Megalithic menhirs were also found placed in many parallel rows, known as alignments. The most famous of these are the ones in Carnac, France, which include nearly 3,000 menhirs. It is thought the alignments were

used for processional rites. These are often pillars or obelisks, up to forty feet (twelve meters) tall.

The third group comprises the *cromlechs*, or henge monuments. These are circular arrangements of megaliths, which probably demarcated areas of cult worship. In some of these, two stones support a third one. The formation is called a *trilith*. One of the best-known megalithic sites is Stonehenge in England. A large circle of stones, connected to each other by cap stones, surrounds a series of five gigantic triliths. These are arranged in a horseshoe shape around a heavy altar stone. Presumed by the placement of the megaliths to do with sun and moon worship, Stonehenge was an indigenous development. Its construction probably covered a few thousand years.

Menhir du Pjessis, Vendée, approximately 112 miles (180 kilometers) southeast of Carnac, France

from burial grounds, not from settlements. The Single-grave people preferred living on ground where organic materials dissolve rapidly.

Puzzles about Prehistoric People
The Bell-beaker society is the final well-known culture of the Neolithic period. Here, too, we are confronted with the fact of how little we actually know about the life of prehistoric people.

What are called cultures in this context are complexes of styles and techniques that show a certain unity and offer a vague picture of the material skills and the burial habits of a people. They bring possibilities, not certainties or proof. The material world and the environment of these prehistoric people can be reconstructed reasonably well by archaeologists, anthropologists, and other specialists. Their religious thinking can only be surmised from what is known about mod-

ern cultures with somewhat similar burial practices or art forms.

Quite a bit of information has been unearthed about the Bell-beaker culture, but an adequate picture of them remains elusive. The Bell-beaker pottery vessels themselves are recognizable enough. They are somewhat similar to the Protruding-foot beakers, but have no bases and are more squat, so that, inverted, they have the shape of a bell. This impression is further reinforced by the decoration of horizontal stripes made by finely toothed stamps. The spread of the Bell-beaker people can be followed by noting stylistic changes in these decorations, suggesting the movement of small mobile groups who might have actively sought out copper and gold. The earliest forms are found on the Iberian Peninsula. From there the Bell-beaker culture spread toward North Africa, Sardinia, and Sicily and via the Rhône Valley, inland to central Europe. Once

Stonehenge in England. A large circle of stones, connected to each other by cap stones, surrounds a series of five gigantic triliths. The placement of the megaliths indicates the probability this was used for sun and moon worship.

Stonehenge from the air

over the Alps, it spread along the Po River through northern Italy and, through Bavaria, along the Rhine River to central Germany, Hungary, and Poland. Important centers have been found in Bohemia and Moravia. Bell-beaker culture reached Bretagne, Belgium, and the Netherlands by way of sea routes in approximately 2000 BC.

Trade Hypotheses
Evidence exists of the rapid spread of Bell-beaker culture elsewhere, but there is no evi-

Interior of a Megalithic gallery-tomb near Antequera, Málaga, Spain

dence of their migration. Their influence was probably due to the copper daggers they made. They are called tongue daggers because of the part that fastens the blade to the handle. These daggers are of great importance. The Bell-beaker people were the first in western Europe to have knowledge of metal processing.

While the people working the land in far-off areas of the temperate zone were restricted to using stone, metallurgy was already being used in parts of Iberia and southeastern Europe. The smelting of copper from copper ore was a turning point in the history of technology. Now mankind was able to produce new materials, and in order to do so the human race had to leap ahead well beyond flint. It did not surprise archaeologists to find

that literacy and metallurgy were found together at the same site. It has commonly been assumed that when a sophisticated ability such as metallurgy appeared in the prehistoric societies we would classify as barbarian, it can only be explained in terms of their contact with early centers of civilization.

Once it was established that prehistoric humans were capable of moving large distances over land and sea, it was assumed that the Bell-beaker people had been tradesmen. It was known that they traveled throughout Europe. Their merchandise was originally assumed to consist of copper tools. This would correlate well with their beginnings in Spain and their later flourishing in Bohemia, both metal-rich areas. However, there are very few findings of the copperware that would have been expected among their customers, the people in their neighboring areas. Since no group of people could have subsisted on such limited trade, the search continued for what else they might have traded. Scientists began to look for some form of perishable goods. Bell-beaker contact with Portugal and Bretagne led to an acceptable hypothesis: salt. The agricultural peoples of Europe would have required large amounts of salt and the Bell-beaker people, it was theorized, could have brought it to them. This was a clever assumption, but one that could not be entirely substantiated. Remnants of Bell-beaker culture were found at places where any transport of salt by sea would have been impossible. Hence, it must be assumed that Bell-beaker culture was not as specialized as these hypotheses would imply.

The Bell-beaker settlements show the normal pattern of Neolithic mixed industry. It is known that they did metal processing and preferred to settle at places where copper could be found. People in their settlements elsewhere probably obtained copper from their tribal relatives. Bell-beaker people everywhere were good potters, in addition to being skilled metal-processors. They probably traded along the large rivers. Based on the striking characteristics of their handicraft, it can also be deduced that they crossed from Europe to England and Ireland. They made a modest start there in the Bronze Age.

The Naveta des Tudons, a Neolithic settlement on the island of Menorca in Spain. These and similar buildings were probably used as collective graves.

The Bronze Age

Revealing the Possibilities of Metal

The major changes that occurred over the Neolithic period completely altered human life. More changes followed at increasingly short intervals. The period of discovery had begun. By the end of the Neolithic era, people were familiar with peas, flax (the plant from which linen is made), and the most important types of grain. In the Americas, potatoes and maize were known. The digging stick and the hoe had long been supplemented by the "drag cart," the forerunner of the plow. By this time cattle were drawn to the plow, yoked in pairs. In some regions, cattle were already being replaced by the much stronger oxen. These animals were generally castrated so that people could more

91

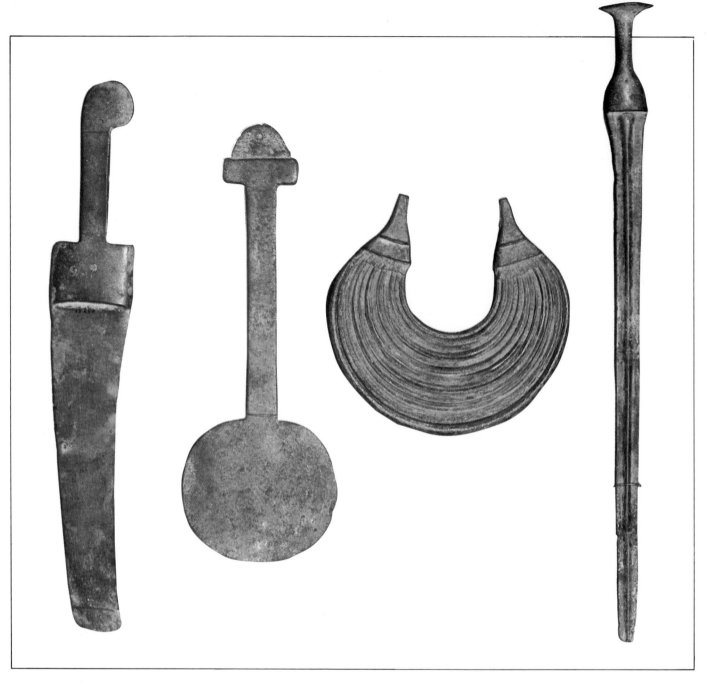

Bronze sword,
mirror, dagger, and collar
found near Lloseta on
Mallorca, Spain

easily control them. Draft oxen were found in Europe as early as the Funnel-beaker culture. Other tribes had succeeded in domesticating donkeys for use in pulling or carrying loads.

The function of the horse at this time is not clear. Neolithic cave paintings show horses mainly as highly prized game, but some could also have been used as beasts of burden. In the beginning people probably raised horses for meat and for mares' milk. There are no clear indications that they were used for riding prior to 3000 BC.

The ancestry of the horse is one of the clearest lineages in all of paleontology. The horse family, known as *Equidae*, began during the Eocene epoch, which lasted from about 54 million to 38 million years ago. During the early Eocene, the first example of the horse appeared, a mammal that browsed

and was hoofed, known as Hyracotherium, but more commonly known as Cohippus, the "dawn horse." Fossils of this animal have been found in both Europe and North America, and show that it stood only from 4.2 to 5 hands (2.5–4 inches or 6.4–10.2 centimeters) high, with raised hindquarters and a back that arched. There were padded feet at the ends of the legs, with four functional hooves on the forefeet and three on the back. The brain was far smaller and less complex, and the teeth were that of a browser. The dawn horse was so unlike the modern horse that it wasn't recognized as a horse at all at first. Only when paleontologists found fossils of later extinct horses did it become clear that there was a link to eohippus.

Horses had evolved from the dog-sized, four-toed *Eohippus*, through the larger three-toed *Mesohippus*, to the single-toed

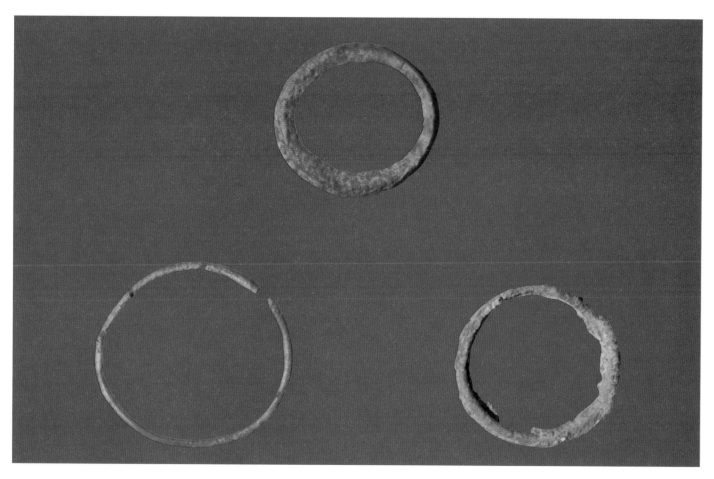

Bronze bracelets
from the El Argar culture,
found in Almeria,
Spain. Early Bronze Age,
c.1600 BC.

Merychippus of 25 million years ago. The still larger *Pliohippus* of 12 to 2 million years ago was the immediate predecessor of the *Equus*, the Neolithic horses then in existence in Eurasia. The predominant species was the tarpan (classified as *Equus caballus gmelini*). A small wild horse, only recently extinct, it is identified by some zoologists with the Przevalsk horse, which still exists. It had a sturdy body set on short legs and averaged 4 to 5 feet (1.2 to 1.5 meters) at shoulder height. Tarpans were usually gray with black manes and tails. Wild bands of them were slaughtered in the nineteenth and early twentieth centuries in Europe because of the danger they presented to crops and to the modern breeds of horses that had long ago evolved from them. The horse we know today went through many changes in its evolution from the small dawn horse. The evolution includes an increase in size, fewer hooves, loss of the foot pads, a lengthening of the legs, the fusion of the independent bones of the lower legs, muzzle elongation, increase in brain mass and development of teeth fit for grazing.

New Means of Transport

The displacement of Neolithic farming people forced a concomitant increase in the need for a ready means of transport. These people did not roam the forests in the manner of the Mesolithic hunters and gatherers, but occasionally they did have to relocate to new agricultural ground. They required a means of hauling loads for this and for use in their regular work. To solve the problem, they developed a type of primitive sled, the first method of transportation. Such sleds were adopted for use by hunters as well.

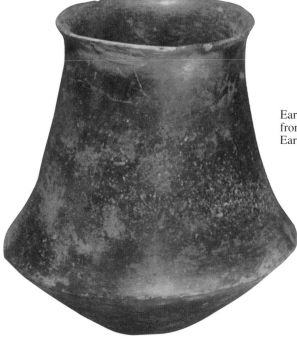

Earthenware pot
from the El Argar culture.
Early Bronze Age

93

Stone houses
on the Scottish island
of Skara Brae

In Eurasia people began to use lengths of tree trunks as rollers for transporting particularly burdensome material. It is probable that the invention of the wheel stemmed from those rolling tree trunks. The discovery of the wheel was probably made by the steppe people in northern Mesopotamia around 3500 BC. The invention spread rapidly through Eurasia. The development of carts had an immeasurable effect on mankind. Greatly increasing the mobility of the farming tribes, it was part of the reason why Neolithic civilization could spread so quickly.

The people of the Mesolithic had already hollowed out tree trunks to make canoes. Neolithic people made other small boats made with wooden frameworks covered with

Wooden and Stone Tribal Dwellings

As far back as the *bandkeramik* culture, people had been building quite large longhouses with walls made of woven fiber covered with clay. Less often, the walls were made of poles driven close together into the ground, or constructed of wooden panels.

In Switzerland and adjacent areas, unusual Neolithic houses called "pike dwellings" have been found. Ingeniously designed, they stood on pikes above swampy ground. The supporting pikes were driven deep into the swampy ground, right on top of each other, until they rested on solid ground. The technique made it possible for people to live in wetland areas near the sea. Various theories were advanced as to why they were built so high above the water. It is now known that water levels have dropped since they were constructed.

In other locations, where wood was scarce, people built houses of stone, coral, or other materials they found available. Houses in Jericho, the earliest Neolithic settlement

Two examples of Palestinian earthenware from the middle of the Bronze Age

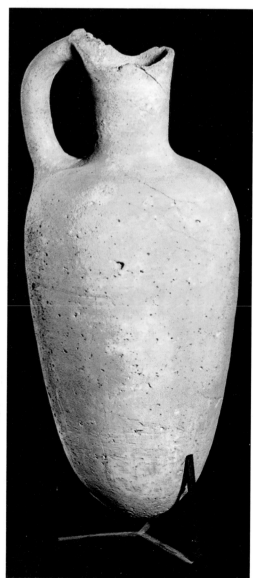

hide. It is not known exactly when people began to make ships, but certainly the Egyptians had them by 4000 BC. There is evidence that shortly afterward they became also familiar with the sail. The oldest Egyptian ships were made of bunches of papyrus material. By 3000 BC, sails were in common use throughout the Mediterranean Sea.

The people of the Mesolithic era used hollowed-out tree trunks to make canoes.

known, were built of stone. Those in the ancient city of Catal Hüyük (in Turkey) were made of sun-baked clay bricks. The houses were placed close together over an area of nearly 500,000 square feet (152,400 square meters), with only an occasional small square or inner courtyard. Openings in the flat roofs served as doors. People entered the houses by means of stairs. Benches set against the walls served as burial vaults for relatives.

There was great emphasis on tribal relationships in the Neolithic settlements. Entire tribes lived together in enormous houses. The great house in Jutland (Denmark) was one such tribal dwelling. On the Scottish island Skara Brae, stone houses were connected to each other by hallways. In this settlement, everything was made of stone, even the cupboards and the beds. The entire complex was managed by formidable defense towers reminiscent of those at Jericho. Such labyrinthine blocks of housing are also found among the Pueblo Indians in America.

Although they may have formed the architectural groundwork for the large urban cultures of Mesopotamia, Egypt, and Mexico, these Neolithic settlements were not actually cities. They were simply the homes of whole tribes or clans.

Craftsmen and Specialists

The rapid development of the art of pottery made fundamental changes in human life. It provided a new means of storage in addition to the rawhide bags, gourds, horns, and straw baskets already in use. Even the earliest clay pots were probably decorated with carvings of some sort. As techniques improved, it is probable that professional potters emerged. In Egypt and Korea, precursors of the pottery wheel have been found that date from before the Bronze Age. They were probably used by specialized individuals with highly specialized skills.

Petroglyphs (paintings in rock wall and in caves) dating from the Neolithic era have not been found in Europe, but sculpture evidently reached a new level in that period. In addition to the continuation of traditional realism, there was a strong emphasis on representation and style. The work is abstract, its focus completely on a few important characteristics of the creature illustrated. Some female figurines from that period are so stylized as to take on the character of symbols or signs. They became schematic illustrations of the concepts behind them, such as fertility or motherhood. This was a significant step, the first hint of the invention of writing.

The manufacture of certain essential objects fell increasingly to the hands of a few skilled people. This evolution of craftsmanship was very important. The craftspeople provided for their living by trading the objects they made for food or other things they needed made by other specialists. Warriors, priests, and shamans (or medicine men) played specialized roles of growing importance in society. Warriors were probably regarded as necessary for defense, even among cultures not interested in deliberate expansion. Priests and shamans alike would have maintained contact with the supernatural, receiving goods as payments for their services from the communities in which they worked. Their role must have been significant in that period, yet little is known about their specific practices, as they left behind few tangible traces.

Prehistoric Brain Surgery

One of the unique capabilities of Neolithic human was *trepanation*, the removal of a piece of the skull. In prehistoric times, humans probably had no intention of touching the brain itself. Infection of the cerebral membrane and brain tissue would have meant the certain death of the patient. It is evident from the findings of trepanned skulls, which date from the Neolithic period, that the patient typically did survive the operation. The skulls show partial recovery of the bone at the edges of the wound.

The meaning behind the idea of trepanation remains unclear. It is assumed that these early trepanations were done with the objective of driving evil spirits out of the body, thereby combating madness and epilepsy.

The people of the Neolithic were competent at making tools out of bone, and the skills needed for this surgery were similar ones. With flint tools they would cut and drill until they could take out a piece of skull without damaging the brain. The work required an expertise that only certain highly specialized shamans possessed. The pieces of bone taken out of the skull were often round and worn as amulets. The oldest evidence of trepanation is some 2,000 years old. The custom continued to the early Middle Ages in Europe, where trepanned skulls have been found from Russia to the Netherlands. (Most of these operations were done during the Neolithic Age within the Single-grave culture, but none were done among the Bell-beakers.) A trepanned mummy was discovered in Egypt, and trepanation still occurs in Africa. It was also known in South America. Over a thousand trepanned skulls have been unearthed from the Inca civilization of Peru.

Metal *versus* Stone

It is certainly not an exaggeration to speak of a "Neolithic revolution." The Neolithic peri-

Trepanned skull from the La Pastora cave near Alicante, Spain

od brought human beings a large number of innovations within a very short period of time. The most important of these included the domestication of the llama in America and of the zebu and other poultry in southeastern Asia; the spinning of linen thread from flax and yarn from sheep wool and goat hair; weaving; the intense utilization of date palms and fig and olive trees along the Mediterranean Sea coasts; and cultivation of the grapevine. The making of wine appears to already have been discovered, and beer was made by fermenting barley. Also, the concept of crop fertilization had been discovered and was occasionally put to use.

Despite the importance of these innovations in agriculture, animal husbandry, and textiles, the most significant accomplishment of the Neolithic period was the development of metallurgy. It must be pointed out that none of these changes occurred over a short period of time. From the modern point

97

Losa, a Megalithic settlement
on Sardinia.
Late Bronze Age,
c.1000 BC.

of view, prehistoric cultures took a long time
to adopt new lifestyles. The use of metal
began so gradually that its starting point can
hardly be ascertained. Yet by a certain time
its role had become so important to society
that the era must be called the Bronze Age.
There were, of course, local variations in the
use of metal.

The Bronze Age began much earlier in
some regions and cultures than in others. A
few small copper objects have been recovered from as early as the Funnel-beaker culture, more than 2,000 years ago. Others were
found from the later Bell-beaker culture. To
the surprise of many experts, metal has been
found in a few recently excavated settlements dating from the early Neolithic period.
In both Cayonu and Catal Hüyük (in
Turkey), simple utility objects made of hammered copper have been found. These settlements are two of the oldest of the Neolithic

period. Among the objects found in them
were picks, needles, and rolls of copper wire
that may have been used as bracelets or
something similar. These cultures were otherwise purely Neolithic. Their essential tools
were made of flint, obsidian, or bone.

These settlements lend credence to
the view of some historians, who present
the concept of a "Copper Age" preceding the
Bronze Age. There is no one specific beginning point of the Bronze Age, but consider it
to span the period from 3000 BC to approximately 800 BC.

By definition, the Neolithic period begins
at the moment when humans first began to
plant seeds. The Bronze Age, in contrast,
cannot be said to have begun with the first
processing of metal. On the other hand, at
that first moment of seeding, Neolithic
achievements were certainly not universal.
Older practices continued to coexist with the

Neolithic Ice Man

Many great archaeological sites have been discovered by chance. In 1940 a tree was uprooted near where four French schoolboys were playing. When they investigated a shaft at the base of the hole they found themselves in the midst of the famous Upper Paleolithic cave paintings in Lascaux, southern France. Similarly, a body was discovered in September of 1991, by hikers in the Tirolean Alps. The corpse, still half covered with ice, lay in a hollow at an elevation of 10,000 feet (3,048 meters). It turned out to be the body of a 5,500-year-old man.

This unique discovery gives significant insight into prehistoric human life, particularly around 3000 BC. This "ice man" has been called Similaun man (after the glacier on which he was found) or Oetzi (after the mountain where the glacier was located).

He had died at approximately the age of thirty. His body was remarkably well preserved and tattooed on the back with vertical lines. Their function is unclear. His clothes and the things he had carried with him were also well preserved.

Oetzi was dressed in fur that was leather-sewn. He wore a leather and fur cap and a poncho made of woven grass. His boots were lined with hay and bound with laces of grass and leather. His equipment was well chosen for a journey through the mountains. He carried a hatchet, a bow and a quiver, and a leather backpack that held oak leaves, a flint fire-starter, and a dagger.

The hatchet is remarkable in that it is made of copper and of a very early type. It was set in a taxus (wood of the yew tree) handle approximately 30 inches long (about 76 centimeters). His half-finished bow was also made of taxus and measured some 6 feet (almost 2 meters) long. His leather quiver contained fourteen wooden arrow shafts, each about 33 inches (84 centimeters long). Two arrows were ready for use, already fitted with flint arrowheads and feathers. The quiver also contained a pointed tool made of antler, probably a punch used to retouch flint blades and arrowheads, and a sinew of an animal.

The backpack consisted of a long leather bag on a hazelnut frame. It contained a flint scraper, a birch sheath, and pieces of pyrite, all equipment used to start a fire. It also held two spare flint arrowheads, material for processing flint, two pieces of fungus sewn onto a leather belt, and a dagger. The dagger was flint affixed to a wooden grip. It was kept in a sheath of woven grass.

The ice man probably died of exhaustion in the mountains. We are not yet sure what brought him there. From other excavations we know that during that time people regularly went into the mountains to make use of

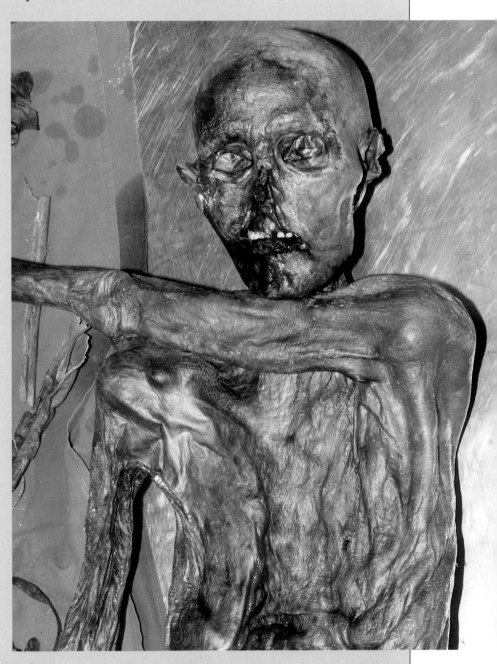

the high pastures. Oetzi could have been a shepherd who met with bad weather, sought shelter, and then died in the hollow of the cliff. Considering the material he had with him, he could also have been a hunter or even a warrior.

Oetzi, the body of a 5,500-year-old man, found in the Tirolean Alps in September, 1991

Mold that was used
for bronze axes,
from Mola Alta de Serelles,
Alicante, Spain

Bronze sword from
the Late Bronze Age found
in Brandon East Hill
near Glanton,
England.

new for a long time.

During the Bronze Age in Europe, trade and crafts specialization began assuming a more important place in society, but otherwise the lifestyle of the Bronze Age does not differ significantly from that of the Neolithic period. In the Near East, the Bronze Age was coupled with a new direction for society, an urban revolution in Mesopotamia and Egypt. Just as the Neolithic era was influenced by the Mesolithic in its development of agriculture, so the Bronze Age rests on the foundation of the Neolithic period. People of that period could increasingly rely on stable food supplies under their own management. They no longer needed to spend the majority of their time in meeting their basic living requirements. Methods of storage had improved. Domesticated animals were always available.

It became possible for Neolithic people to use their time to experiment. The use of metal, at that point, approximately 6000 BC, was uncommon. It was only by accident that people used it at all. They generally did so only when copper was found in the area, on the surface of the ground. The fantastic possibilities of metals were not yet comprehended and could not yet be realized technically.

The Development of Copper Processing

Up to now we have used the terms *metal*, *copper*, and *bronze* indiscriminately. To differentiate, copper is a reddish brown malleable, ductile metallic element. It is found around the world in ores (chacopyrite and bornite are the most common). The fact that it also occurs in the pure state in nature is the reason for its early use. The island of Cyprus has so much of it that the metal was named for the island, *Kyprios* in Greek. (The chemical symbol of the element is Cu, from the Latin contraction of the name *cuprus*.) Copper is relatively soft. A lump of it can be shaped by hammer even when it is cold. In this process, the copper gets harder and becomes brittle. Continued hammering (for example, to make a knife blade) can crack the metal and render the object too fragile for use.

In order for copper to be processed, it must be made red-hot and then tempered, cooled off immediately in cold water. The tempering makes the copper soft enough to be processed without cracking. Hardness is regained through hammering (called "work hardening"). It is sometimes necessary to repeat the process several times to achieve the shape and hardness desired for tool use.

This technique may have been discovered from the cooking practice called "immersion technique," which involved bringing water to a boil by putting red-hot stones in it. (The water might have been poured into a hide bag or bark container or found in the hollow of a rock.) It is a technique used by some modern people as well as prehistoric. It is quite possible that someone used chunks of copper as cooking stones and discovered that the metal could then be processed much more easily.

The greatest advantage of metal is its capacity to be formed, but this characteristic cannot be used to full advantage through cold hammering. Only through casting, the melting and molding of metal, can its full potential be realized. The melting point of copper is 1,981°F (1,083°C), so in an ordinary open fire it would never melt. It can be melted only when temperature is increased by blowing into the fire (by means of a bellows) or using an oven. The most telling explanation for the fact that Neolithic people wanted to achieve such high temperatures is that they noticed that it improved the quality of fired earthenware. The discovery that

Several bronze
swords and spearheads
from Wittingham
Hoard, 600 BC

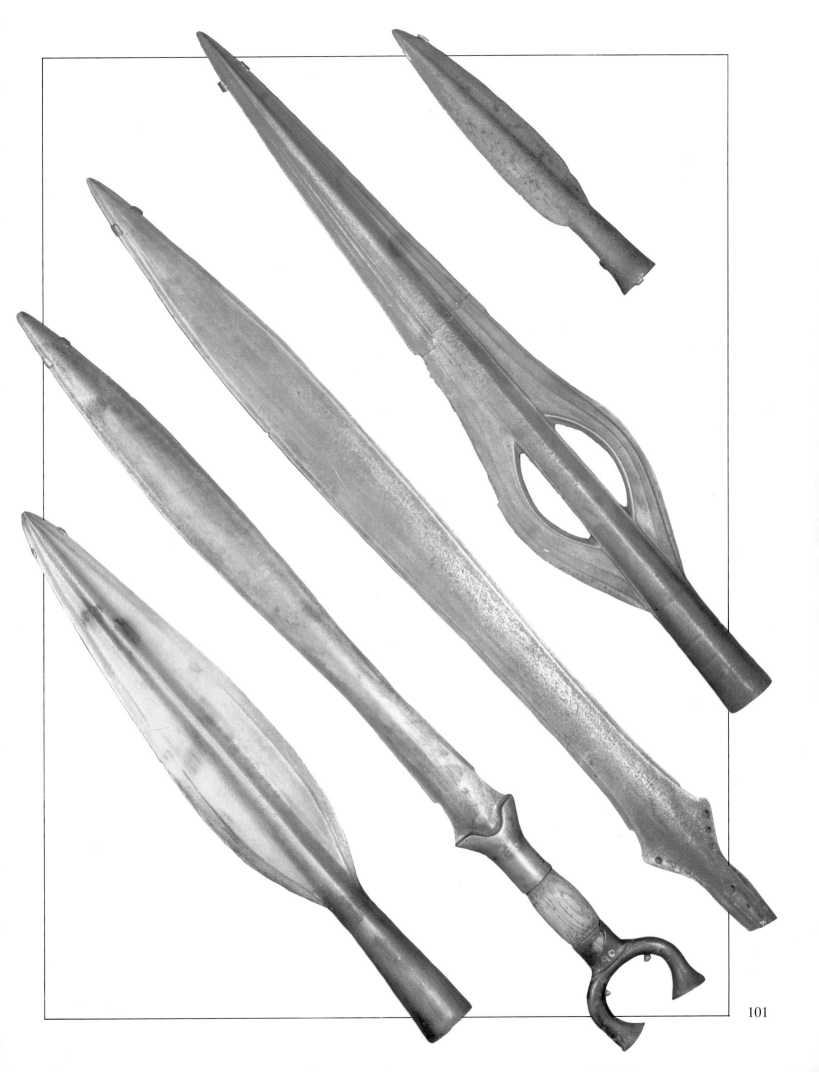

copper could melt was thus associated with pottery making. Human perception of accidental occurrences, coupled with repeated experimentation, probably led to the development of the art of casting. The first molds were probably hollowed rock. (It is interesting to note, in this context, that the settlement of Cayonu was not familiar with earthenware and used hollowed-out stones as containers.) Hammered copper could, be preceramic, but cast copper could not.

Part of a waist belt of hammered bronze from Paransot Moidon, France

A number of important types of tools were typically cast of copper: hatchets, adzes, chissels, knives, and pickaxes. They were poured into a rough mold, then finished and hardened by hammering.

The development of copper processing took many centuries, from at least 6,000 to approximately 3,000 years ago. In the central part of Asia Minor, for centuries a sort of "Copper Age" existed that preceded the Bronze Age. Between 4000 and 3000 BC, copper was introduced in the Balkan areas, and a bit later in southern Russia, too. Copper objects have also been recovered from ancient cultures in Egypt, Crete, China, and, of course, Cyprus. Copper was familiar to Native Americans, as well. In North America, pure copper can be found in great quantities. There are many accessible surface deposits in the area of Lake Superior. The Indians learned to work copper, but never mastered the art of casting. Metal processing appears to have made its appearance in the New World around the beginning of the common era, c. AD 100.

The manufacture of alloys followed the development of casting. This involves the blending or melting together of various metals. Alloys of copper are far harder and stronger than pure copper. Tin is added to molten copper to form bronze, the earliest alloy of copper. Zinc is added to form brass. Both tin and zinc can be added to the same alloy, so no sharp distinction can be made between brass and bronze.

People in the Bronze Age also began to process gold. Like copper, it is found in nature in a pure form as well as in a combined state in ore. It can be taken from quartz veins and alluvial deposits, but seldom in large chunks or significant quantities. Again like copper, it is widely distributed on Earth but is much more rare than copper. It is generally found with some amount of silver. An alloy of gold and silver called electrum occurs naturally. (Gold also occurs in combination with other minerals: calaverite and sylvanite. With lead, antimony, and sulfur, it forms nagyagite. With mercury, it forms gold amalgam. It is more obvious in iron pyrite, called "fool's gold," and is also in galena, the lead sulfide ore of silver. Minute amounts of gold are even in seawater.) From the very beginning, gold was valuable. In the New World, gold is found in larger quantities, and there it began to play a great role in the classical Mayan and Inca cultures.

The Bronze Age person probably panned for gold in much the same way as the prospectors in the American Old West, swishing gold-bearing sand and water in a shallow pan of some sort until the lighter sand washed out and left the heavier grains of gold behind.

Because of its softness, which makes it completely unsuitable for tools, gold can be processed easily. Thin pieces of gold were hammered into thin sheets and applied as gold leaf. Because gold is only found in small pieces, larger golden objects could not be made until the development of smelting.

The Trundholm Chariot of the Sun god. One side of the sun disk is covered with gold leaf, which is decorated with a spiral motif. Early Bronze Age c.1400–1200 BC

Developing Use of Metals

Prehistoric Mining

The use of copper and alloys of copper, such as bronze, was the point at which the Stone Age became the Metal Age. Copper was one of the first metals ever used by humankind. From the beginning of recorded history until the medieval period it was the world's most useful metal, a great improvement over wood and stone. Copper was used for tools, utensils, ornaments, arrowheads, statues, and more. It is one of the best conductors of heat and electricity.

During the Upper Paleolithic period, probably around 10,000 BC, Neolithic people discovered the existence of copper and started to use it. Copper may have been discovered through the common practice of pulverizing colored minerals for use as decorative pigments. They used the green mineral malachite and the blue mineral azurite, both copper-containing ores. These did not pulverize under the hammer: they bent. The tiny bits of copper found in them were soon put to use, at least in jewelry.

Neolithic people used native copper or copper in a free metallic state. It could be hammered, which made it harder and able to

Necklace consisting
of beads of amber and
faience found in a necropolis,
Middle Bronze Age

Bronze sickles from
the Early and Middle Bronze
Ages, respectively

hold an edge but more brittle. (This is called *work hardening*.) They probably also discovered that if they repeatedly hammered the copper and then heated it in fire, it would not crack. This process of relieving metal stress is called *annealing*.

At about 6000 BC it was discovered that copper could be melted by fire and then cast into a desired shape, using a mold. This eliminated much of the hammering that had previously been required. Findings at Rudna Glavna, Serbia, show that copper was in use there in 4000 BC. The casting technology led to improvements in pottery since it was used in molds.

Other evidence in Europe, dating from around 3000 BC, indicates that people gradually began to utilize mineral ores rather than just the elements copper and gold, which they had been able to find occurring naturally in a pure state. (Silver, lead, and tin virtually never occur in their pure form.) This step created a simultaneous increase in the assortment of metals used.

The incentive for the development may have been the lucrative manufacture of copper tools. These tools, so much more superior than those made of stone or wood, had to have been very much in demand. The need for new sources of copper probably increased interest in new methods of utilizing the copper found in less pure ore.

No one knows how the next stage in the use of copper was discovered. Copper ore, which is not useful in its natural state, will yield metallic copper when heated to a temperature higher than that found in a normal campfire. This production of metal from ore is called *smelting*. A combination of events had to happen and be noticed for progress to occur.

A further improvement in the smelting process was the roasting of the copper ore prior to smelting. This separated the copper from some of its impurities and converted the copper in the ore to copper oxide.

The first copper ore processed was an arsenic-containing compound. The presence of the arsenic in the ore was a hindrance. Like any impurity, it had to be eliminated to make casting the copper possible. Like the sulfur that occurs in certain types of copper ore, it could be removed by roasting. The ore was heated in the open air to drive off the sulfur and oxidize the copper. The copper oxide was then converted, by smelting, into metallic copper. This was done in a clay oven covered with clay lids. Alternating layers of copper oxide, ore, and charcoal were placed in the oven. It was then heated to a red-hot temperature with the aid of a bellows.

The copper accumulated at the bottom of the oven. The purity of that copper could be increased by removing the ash that rose to the top. The small impurities that still occurred varied with the type of ore that had been used. By following the traces of this process, modern investigators can determine the origin of various ores by analyzing products they find.

The Forging Trade

It is clear that such a complicated treatment of raw materials must have been the work of specialized craftsmen. The first smiths probably looked for their own copper and then processed it. Once ore mining began on a larger scale, a division of labor was required. Some people dug up the ore; others smelted it. Still others were responsible for the charcoal and the delivery and removal of waste products from the ore. Eventually, complete mining centers developed. Their production was intended for export as well as local use.

Since the people lacked any means of transporting ore in large quantities, the processed metal had to be cast on site. Modern versions of such processed metal are formed as loaflike bars called ingots. The prehistoric metal was cast in nearly closed rings. Holes, like the eyes of needles, were cut into each end. Rope was threaded through them in order to tie the rings onto pack animals for transport. The metal cutouts from the holes were either smelted down again or reprocessed to make miniature rings used as money. Each replica ring had a certain value. The rings were often worn as necklaces, and similar rings are still worn today in the African interior. Cutouts from the mountain country of central Europe were traded actively around 2000 BC in Denmark and Syria. Metalsmiths fashioned them into decorative and utilitarian objects.

The smiths played an extensive role in the spread of the metal culture, teaching the craft to their sons, who would then move away and begin working independently elsewhere. Local assistants were often employed to operate the bellows and assist in other work. These helpers sometimes managed to learn the craft by watching their employers, and then moving on to work elsewhere.

Traveling metalworkers went to many areas, offering their special skills. The extensive trade networks that already existed during the Neolithic period also provided market knowledge and geographic information. Communities knew where there was work for a good craftsman, whether he was a smith or a potter. They also knew where ore might be found in the mountains. It is quite unlikely that the Bell-beaker culture, specializing in metal, was found in both the central European mountains and England. They

Bronze swords and a spearhead, from a necropolis

Most Important European Cultures of the Bronze Age

found copper in the first area and the tin they needed for the manufacture of bronze in the other.

The Early Bronze Age

The term *Bronze Age* is really only of local significance. Bronze was first used and then replaced by iron at varying times in various cultures of the world. The term signifies the primary use of bronze for tools and weapons. Almost always, however, it followed a cultural Copper Age.

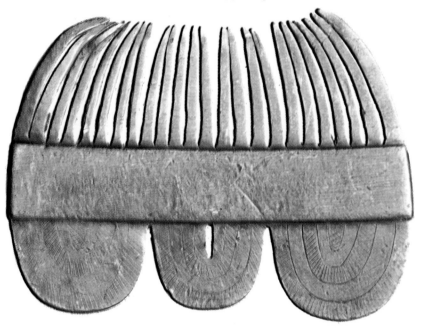

Gold comb from the treasure trove of Caldas de Reyes, Pontevedra, Spain. Middle Bronze Age

According to the prevailing archaeological wisdom prior to 1960, bronze technology had been thought to originate in the Near East. Recent discoveries near Ban Chiang, Thailand, reveal the use of bronze around 4500 BC, preceding its use in the Middle East by several hundred years. Bronze objects have been found in Asia Minor and Greece that date from before 3000 BC, but it took more than a thousand years before the alloy made its way to Europe. In China, it was in common use about 1800 BC. In the Americas, a bronze age began about AD 1000.

In the Mediterranean region, including the Middle East, the Bronze Age has been categorized as having three phases, based on the degree to which the metal was used. The early phase included the Sumerian culture in Mesopotamia and the famed treasures of Troy. The middle phase was epitomized by Babylonian culture, and the late phase by Minoan Crete and Mycenaean Greece. After about 1200 BC, Bronze Age technology in the Mediterranean regions yielded to that of iron.

Bronze Technology

Bronze is any of several alloys, typically consisting of nine parts copper and one part tin, frequently in combination with several other metals. It is stronger than any other alloy except steel, and it cannot rust. By mix-

Interment in an urn was one of the ways of burial which were used in the El Argar culture during the Early Bronze Age.

106

ing the metals, a new one is created that is harder and easier to work than its separate components. The constituents of bronze vary historically with the intended uses of the finished product and the culture. The Greeks and the Romans added zinc, lead, and silver for use in coins, tools, weapons, and objects of art. (These metals are still used in modern bronze.) The hardness of the alloy varies with its components: when it comprises at least 10 percent tin, it is quite hard and yet has a low melting point, making it useful in casting. Different alloys of bronze are given the name of the major constituent metal used in them (for example, aluminum bronze).

The Spread of Bronze

At first bronze was used primarily for decorative purposes. Tin is far rarer than copper, and the supplies needed to make bronze were not available in the regions where the technique developed. Tin is found in large quantities in Europe and England. The Middle East imported tin from Cornwall during the second millennium BC, though there is recent archaeological evidence that suggests that tin may have been mixed in what is now Turkey during the Bronze and Iron Ages. This would certainly have influenced possible trade routes. By the Bronze Age, trade in tin between the Aegean Sea area and the east coast of Spain was long established. Settlements have been found in Iberia that, by their thick walls and towers of "dry plaster" (carefully stacked stones without mortar between them), give clear evidence of their Aegean origins.

The Aegean seamen undoubtedly came to find copper ore. They brought both knowledge of metalworking and the mystery of bronze. Under their influence, a copper-based culture called Almeria developed, which, in turn, later influenced its environment. Because tin was also found in Spain, a Bronze Age can be identified in the El Argar culture around 1700 BC.

The spread of bronze through the rest of

107

Europe probably took place via the trade routes. Again, special note must be taken of the Bell-beaker people, who maintained a certain amount of contact with the El Argar culture in southern Spain. Traces of their presence have been found in such places as the Po Plain and in central Europe. The trade routes of the Bell-beaker culture continued to exist for many centuries. We have been able to reconstruct one of these routes. It ran from the Baltic Sea region via central Europe, where metal could be found, over the Brenner Pass to Italy. From there, most goods were transported to Greece and the Near East.

The first great Bronze Age culture of Europe, the Unetician, is centered around the metal-rich areas of Moravia and Bohemia.

Bronze axe
from Luristan, Persia.
Late Bronze Age.

The Taula de Trepuco,
a Megalithic construction
on Menorca, Spain.
Bronze Age.

108

Pots from Kalenderberg, earthenware found in the Netherlands in the Late Bronze Age. These pots, decorated with fingerprints and by palette knives, were used for domestic purposes.

This culture (called *Aunjetitz* in German) covered a large area in what is today the former Czechoslovakia, Hungary, Austria, and southern Germany. Its peak occurred between 1800 and 1500 BC. Among the most common finds from the area are amber from the Baltic and faience beads from Egypt. These are the items found at the beginning and the end of the great trade route. Unetician products (eyelets, weapons, and jewelry) have been found as far away as the Ukraine and Scandinavia, but they are

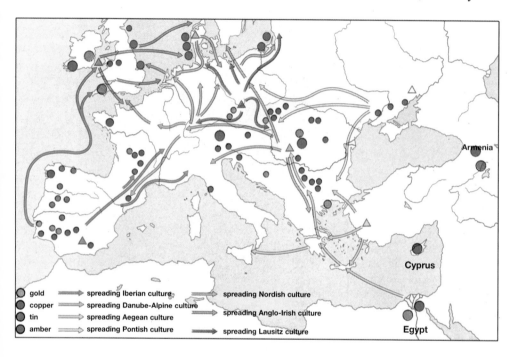

gold	spreading Iberian culture	spreading Nordish culture	
copper	spreading Danube-Alpine culture		
tin	spreading Aegean culture	spreading Anglo-Irish culture	
amber	spreading Pontish culture	spreading Lausitz culture	

Development
of Trade in the European
Bronze Age

seldom found west of the Elbe River. Other cultural groups that were unable to acquire large amounts of bronze lived there.

Scarcity in Northwest Europe

Metal objects remained quite scarce in northwest Europe during the early Bronze Age. Originally the hatchets, spear tips, and pikes (a combination of spear and battle-ax) made elsewhere only trickled into this region. Arrowheads, knives, and blades continued to be made of stone. The flint blades, used as sickles, continued to be especially popular, even once people had access to metal and knew its uses. On the other hand, bronze was so highly esteemed that some flint swords were made as copies of a bronze model. These were among the most impressive flint weapons ever made. It appears as though the flint processors (called *knappers*) were attempting in their work to compete with the popularity of the metalsmiths. These weapons were made in Scandinavia and then traded farther south. By 1700 BC, bronze was in common use in this entire area.

This was true, as well, in the Elp culture, a variant of the burial mound (*tumulus*) culture

in Germany. These people lived in large farmhouses, averaging some 140 feet (about 43 meters) long. Each consisted of a central section and two lateral sections. The house was divided in half to separate the living and the working quarters. The use of metal was probably a vital status symbol in this culture. A bronze hatchet, bronze arrowheads, and golden earrings have been recovered from an Elp grave dating from 1300 BC. The Elp culture continued to thrive for centuries.

During the Bronze Age, there were cultures in existence all over Europe, some of which were very complex. Extensive finds from this era reveal a wealth of contacts and influences from a wide range of sources. The "worldwide" character of the Bronze Age made it possible for all kinds of ideas and techniques to spread easily. One of these was the use of *tumuli* (burial mounds), increasingly popular in numerous cultures. Most of the mounds had the common feature of being surrounded by ring-shaped enclosures, sometimes trenches, ramparts, rows of stones or poles, or a combination of these.

The mounds contained burial gifts, evidently for the dead to take with them for use in the next world. The graves of people assumed to have been military leaders have been found, the deceased buried fully adorned with weapons, clothing, and jewelry. Much later, other people, taken to be the equivalent of royalty, were buried with chariots of war and ships. Also, later in the Bronze Age, people abandoned the age-old habit of burying the dead in a sleeping or sitting position, preferring instead to inter them on their backs.

In apparent contradiction to these customs, cremation became increasingly popular in the Bronze Age. The ashes of those who died were placed in urns and buried. Some of the sites were marked by only a low tumulus or some minimal burial gifts in accordance with the older traditions. The use of cremation may be linked in some way to the observances of the sun cult, which began to replace the former fertility rites. Death and fertility may have been regarded as inseparable by the early agriculturists: it has been observed that the ground was first plowed before a burial mound was constructed.

Decorated Kerbschnitt urn
from the Late Bronze Age, found
in the urnfield of Vlodrop
in the Netherlands.
Dead bodies were burned and
the bones and ashes buried
in urns.

Changes

The changes in burial practice reflect deep-rooted changes in the society of the Bronze Age. The possession of bronze, to tell from the evidence of the burial mounds, appears to have been a prerogative of the rich and, hence, the powerful. Bronze objects represented a concrete value. As a matter of speculation, the bronze hatchets, arrowheads, and dual-edged swords of the time may have given power to those who had the resources to own them. Bronze producers probably became rich and able to fortify and defend the villages, which still offer evidence of the bloody battles of the past. Some societies that controlled trade routes may have made themselves rich and then conquered others. Bronze may have created a social division based on wealth. This is all speculative, but certainly there is evidence of rich life for some individuals living in the Bronze Age. This is seen in their clothing, some of which has been identified in the burial mounds of that time. People wore shirts, long and short skirts, and outer garments and coats of particularly finely woven woolen fabrics. Clothing was held together as necessary with *fibulae* (bronze pins) or with carved outer plates.

The most elaborate artistic skills were expressed, understandably, in the field of metalworking. Splendidly decorated swords and knives, kettles and platters, breastplates and helmets have been recovered. In various places, beautifully cast figurines have been found, usually of bronze but sometimes of gold.

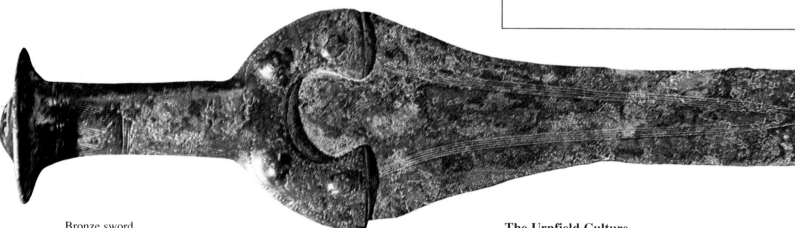

Bronze sword
with rectilinear decorations.
Hallstatt culture.

Earthenware from the Bronze Age has been found in a range of forms and attractive decorative patterns. The art of cave painting once again developed, particularly in Scandinavia. Pictures of farmers, warriors, boats, and animals have yielded a trove of information concerning life in prehistoric times.

The Urnfield Culture

After 1000 BC, a new custom, representative of a culture, spread throughout Europe. Of great significance to the course of history, it is called the Central European Urnfield culture. The name has often led to misunderstanding.

The placement of cremated remains, which distinguishes this culture, was also known in many, much older cultures. These

tion civilizations not only by its urnfields but also by the style of its ceramic vessels and its bronze objects. It is distinguished by bulging mugs with deeply carved decoration, knives with bent backs, and pins with poppy-shaped heads.

Perhaps the origin of the Urnfield culture should be sought in the civilizations of present-day Hungary, where early traces of a cremation culture have been found, but no consensus exists on this point. Early forms of the Urnfield culture came into contact with the burial mound cultures of southern Germany. In this area, at the foot of the Alps, the culture acquired its characteristic properties.

There is evidence that the people of this culture wandered far. They appeared in the villages of the Swiss marshland, traveling via the Rhine Valley through Germany to the Netherlands and eastern England. Their

cultures were related to the Urnfield culture, or were derived from them. There is particular confusion between the Urnfield culture and the Lausitz culture, which was found in a relatively large area of the eastern European plain (modern-day Poland) and its surroundings.

Currently, not all researchers are convinced that the Lausitz represented a separate culture. The Urnfield culture, however, can be differentiated from the other crema-

traces have been found in eastern and southern France, Spain, northern Italy, and Tirol.

Europe on the Move

These migrations took place over a relatively short period of time, between 1200 and 1000 BC. Nonetheless, this migration must not be pictured as the work of a rapidly expanding tribe. No single prehistoric culture in Europe could have initiated such a massive movement. What was involved here

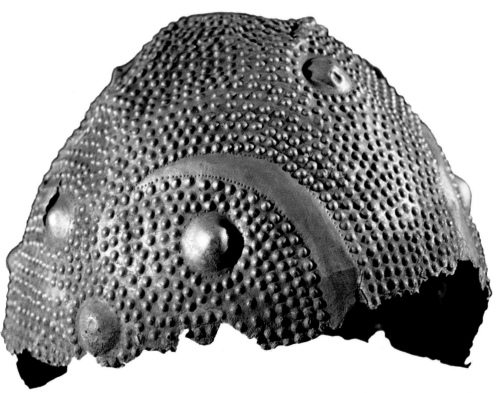

Helmet of embossed silver found in the province of Valencia, Spain. Hallstatt culture, sixth century BC.

was the infiltration of small groups—a few hundred or thousand people—who mixed with the prior inhabitants of an area.

In different places, local variants of the Urnfield culture developed, often mixing with elements of the Tumulus culture. Once such a culture was firmly established at a certain place, a new migration took place. In this case, it is almost certain that what we are dealing with here is a series of migrations, not simply a transfer of cultures from tribe to tribe. Perhaps the most interesting point here is that the migrations of the Urnfield culture, with all their consequences, were not unique.

The Lausitz culture mentioned earlier, between the Oder and the Weichsel in modern-day Germany and Austria, expanded simultaneously eastward and southward. The Balkan region was greatly affected by the invasion. Throughout this region, but particularly in southeastern Europe, heavily fortified cities are encountered from this era. During this same period, as well, Doric invasions took place in Greece, resulting in the destruction of the Mycenaean civilization.

The empire of the Hittite in Asia Minor fell. Egyptian sources from that time complain of invasions from "northern and sea peoples.

It is understandable that large migratory movements have a sort of domino effect, with some peoples pushed aside by others, and the vanquished, in turn, invading neighboring areas. However, it is impossible to identify the first impulse toward the migrations between 1200 and 1000 BC. It has been hypothesized that invasions of nomads from the Russian steppes were responsible for it, but no proof exists. Some scholars point to overpopulation as a factor, which was said to have been a result of the increased agricultural production after the introduction of such technical improvements as the drag cart. That same drag cart made it possible to cultivate heavier and more fertile ground, as well. Others point to the demand for ore-rich areas, toward which the migratory movement was directed. Both factors may be relevant. Still other evidence suggests that Europe and Asia may have experienced a severe climatological change, such as a long-term drought, that forced a change of lifestyle.

Celtic Prehistory

The expansion of the Urnfield culture and related civilizations is significant because this phenomenon is closely related to the origin and spread of the oldest historical cultures in Europe. It is not clear which cultures can be considered forerunners of the Celts. Contenders include the La Tène culture. According to Roman reports, this culture existed from approximately 475 to 440 BC. (Romans called the native Celtic home Gaul.) The La Tène culture undoubtedly developed directly out of the earlier Hallstatt culture, which existed from about 1475 to 1200 BC. It, too, must be viewed as influencing the Celts. The Hallstatt culture existed in the same area as the Urnfield. However, the Urnfield culture cannot be definitely labeled Celtic. One could, at most, state that the people from the Urnfield culture had a certain similarity in style, tradition, and language to the "historic" Celts.

Golden openwork for a varnished bowl from Schwazenbrach, Germany. Celtic art, fifth century BC.

The Iron Age

From the Hittites to the Celts

Although they weren't the first to process iron, the Hittites were the first to dominate a region by using the power they derived from their use of iron. The process of ironworking was considered to be a valuable military secret, one which gave the Hittites an advantage over those with whom they warred, often Mesopotamia and Egypt. The center of the Hittite realm lay in the east of Asia Minor. Its time of greatest influence was around 1500 BC.

The Assyrians from Mesopotamia eventually acquired their own knowledge of iron, and used iron as a means of payment. In their palace of Khorsabad, a stock of 35,000 pounds (16,000 kilograms) of iron has been found in the storehouses.

Among the Egyptians, too, iron was con-

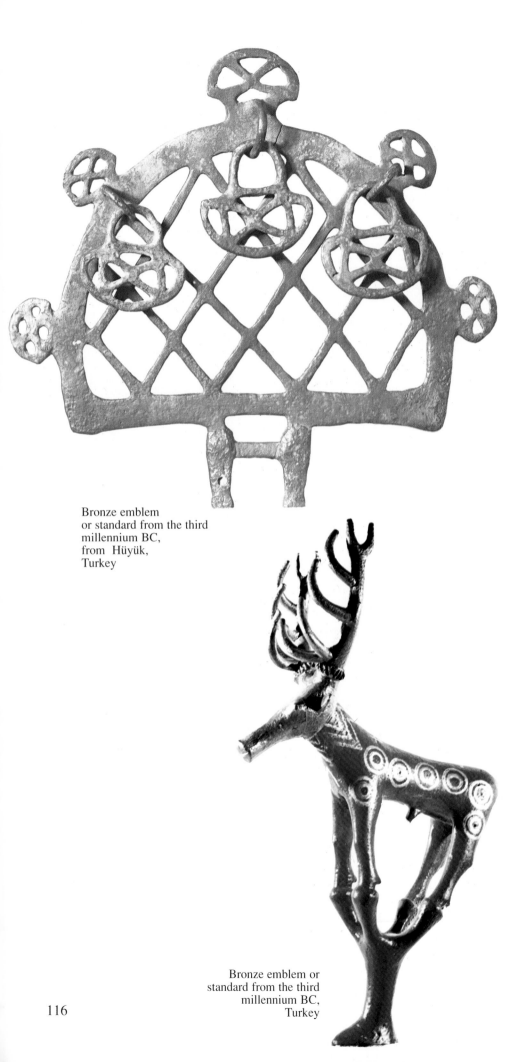

Bronze emblem
or standard from the third
millennium BC,
from Hüyük,
Turkey

Bronze emblem or
standard from the third
millennium BC,
Turkey

sidered to be extremely valuable. There is a well-preserved exchange of letters between the Hittite king Hattusilis III and Pharaoh Ramses II, who reigned about 1250 BC. The letters reveal that after the last great battle at Kadesh (Palestine), an armed peace existed between their two realms. In response to the Pharaoh's request to send him articles made of iron, Hattusilis replied that he was very sorry, but there was no iron left. The reason for this refusal can perhaps be found in the expansion of power of the Hittites to the south. In Syria they had come up against Egyptian interests. The Hittites were so weakened by internal problems that they could offer no resistance to the invasions of what they called the "Sea People," including those from the north.

As early as 2000 BC, tribes in Armenia succeeded in manufacturing usable objects from iron ore. Although ironworking is, to a certain extent, a more complex process than bronze working, the product obtained is nonetheless stronger than bronze. Furthermore, it is also much cheaper to produce, because iron ore is more common than copper—and particularly tin ore. This inexpensive raw material had an enormous social impact, because now it was possible for even small farmers to acquire metal tools. The impact of iron had another significant effect. Iron does not last as long as stone and bronze: it rusts. Iron was also melted down and used over again. At the places where the processing of iron ore had taken place, not a trace of iron has been found. For this reason, certain aspects of the Bronze Age are sometimes better known than those of the early Iron Age.

Around 1000 BC, ironworking spread into the Greek world. The oldest Greek manuscripts from that time mention bronze only in a mythological context. This indicates that iron became a common material quite quickly. After 900 BC we find iron in Italian cultures as well, sometimes together with bronze objects.

At this time there still existed a trade relationship between the Greek-Aegean area and central Europe, a route running through northern Italy. At the terminal end of this route in central Europe we find, around 1000 BC, the Hallstatt culture. In the last century large-scale excavations were carried out in the area of Hallstatt in Austria. Mining technologists uncovered a *necropolis* (city of the dead) located on the site of a mine. In the Austrian Alps, there were settlements, dating back to Paleolithic times, that were based on mining. Despite this, the chief product of Hallstatt is generally conceded to be the salt evident in its name. Since Neolithic times,

salt had been obtained in this area by means of the evaporation of spring water, which contained salt.

In the metal age, shafts were dug into the salt layers. Salt was exported to Italy in exchange for bronze objects (mostly jewelry and luxurious utility objects). For example, Etruscan vases have been found in Hallstatt excavations. In addition, the Hallstatt culture produced its own bronze and iron objects, particularly weapons. Earthenware of the time has also been recovered. In addition to

Bird of fired pottery dating from the middle of the Iron Age

findings of imported Greek vases, there are also indigenous pots and pans. The rich archaeological deposits near Hallstatt consisted of such items as pails and platters of hammered bronze, finely worked bronze trivets and other bases, bronze serving spoons, coat pins, chains, and pendants. Most of this was quite artistic and evidenced considerable skill. Gold objects, too, were common. The indigenous ceramics show stylistic continuity with the Urnfield culture though more ornate in form and on a small

A representation
of a Hittite tradesman

of a type of royal hierarchy within this society. Some figurines and decorations representing warriors are the foundation for this assumption. The knight with his huge dagger and body armor, for instance, represents unmatched power.

Horsemanship held a dominant place in the society of that time. The protection of the fortified villages, which more and more often grew into more extensive fortresses, depended upon the professional soldiers —just as did the safe transport of trade caravans. Goods and payment were the responsibility of the protecting powers, which

Bronze votive chariot with a boar-hunting scene found in Mérida, Spain. Iron Age.

base. The decoration is rich, with multicolored geometric designs, alternating patterned zones and *cannelures* (fluting). Imprinted on the body and neck of some vases are small sculpted figures. Long broadswords were common weapons at this time, made possible by the use of iron. For smaller weapons bronze was still used, but there are also knives, daggers, and lance points made of iron. Iron tubular hatchets, which had to have been molded into shape, give evidence of great technical skill.

Remarkable is the decorative talent with which golden rings and figurines are carved into handles and blades. The Hallstatt culture is thought to have been a wealthy one, although such treasures were only found in the graves of some people. The social differences in the Hallstatt culture were very great. In fact, we can speculate about the existence

became the ruling powers. The best-known example of royal wealth from the Hallstatt culture is found in the grave of Vix in France (Côte d'Or), where a lady of the noble class was buried in a large burial mound. A wagon loaded with treasures was buried along with her. On this well-preserved four-wheeled wagon were found such articles as a bronze *krater* (pitcher) with a splendidly carved rim. This almost five-foot (1.52 meter) vat, weighing over 400 pounds (181 kilograms), originated in Greece. A massive golden diadem weighed nearly a pound (0.45 kilogram); a silver platter and many items of jewelry completed the treasure. At other places where the Hallstatt culture existed, Etruscan bronze work has been found, as well as glassware from Phoenicia and even silk from China. The aristocratic leaders were apparently able to obtain the most

118

Pottery from the Iron Age found in Cortés, Navarra, Spain

refined luxuries from all over the world. In this aspect these oligarchs outdid the leaders of the more democratic Greece, even importing wine from the Mediterranean Sea area and exporting, in turn, slaves. It fit the lifestyle of this top social layer to bury its dead in full dress, chariots and all. This custom was also one of the Asiatic steppe people, who entered regions of the Hallstatt culture from the east and proceeded all the way into Scandinavia.

A People Adrift

The burial customs of the Hallstatt culture are thought to reflect differences in social class. In general, the dead were cremated and then stored according to the traditions of the Urnfield culture. Burial gifts were quite rare, and indeed sometimes no urn was used at all. This may be an indication that the great majority of people of the time were not wealthy enough to afford them, since their trades, agriculture and raising livestock, yielded only a meager living. The people who lived from trade and crafts represented —even in the rich ore areas—a minority. The culture was agrarian, even in the fortified settlements. (There were more urban cultures present in Europe, in those days, notably on the Iberian Peninsula.) The Hallstatt culture expanded from the mountain areas down into the entire region that once had fostered the Urnfield culture. In the south it reached to the Tagus River in Spain,

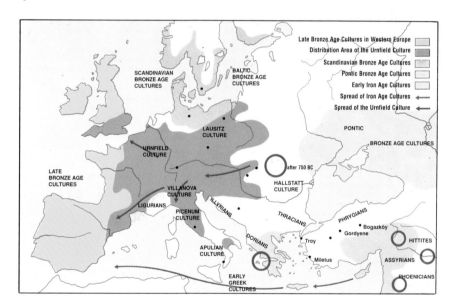

The Rise of Iron in Europe

in the north to the lower Rhine in the Netherlands, and eastward to Hungary. Its influence extended over western France and the northern Balkan. The spread of this culture was not always without conflict. Groups of warriors from the core areas overpowered their neighboring tribes.

In eastern Belgium—in the mountainous areas of the Meuse and Sambre—there existed an indigenous iron industry. The rudimentary manner of ore processing resulted in an enormous amount of waste, leaving large slag heaps behind. These slag heaps can still be seen today, although a large portion of them were reprocessed in historic

119

Fragment of a gold tiara found in Ribadeo. Hallstatt culture.

Knife from the Iron Age

times, making use of the nearly 40 percent iron still present in them. Along these lines, sand piles in the Ardennes still bear witness to the mining of gold by the washing of river sand. The North Sea coast at the border between Belgium and the Netherlands was partially stripped to acquire salt. Evidence of agriculture dating from this period can be identified in several areas, particularly by aerial photos. A network of low walls is visible, enclosing farmlands of 15 to 40 acres (6 to 16 hectares). The strange thing is that the earth, from which these walls were built, was taken out of the fields themselves, but without any traces of ditches left behind. Perhaps the farmers plowed under the top layer of their fields from time to time, a form of farming known in England, where it is called the "Celtic fields" system. Most of these fields probably come from a period after the Hallstatt culture.

Above the great rivers, agricultural cultures like those of the late Bronze Age have been found from this period. Their traditions clearly date back to that time. Iron was scarce, and such a battle-ready elite class as there was in the south did not yet exist here. The society in the north shows, on the contrary, a particularly peaceful character. The Germanics, however, definitely penetrated farther into the south. This is probably associated with the slow deterioration of the southern Scandinavian culture due to the reduction of its trade contacts with central Europe. The Hallstatt people exported nearly all their metal to the Mediterranean Sea area, which offered them higher prices.

The Iberian Culture

Greek civilization had already reached a high point. Like the Phoenicians before them, the Greeks established trading posts for their commercial efforts in Iberia, southern Italy, and Sicily. Often these trading posts expanded to become full-scale colonies. The people with whom the Greeks came in contact developed rapidly under their influence. We have acquired information about these groups from Greece, since they did not yet possess writing skills.

The people of this Iberian culture in the non-Celtic part of Spain and southern France took much from the Greeks. However, their indigenous culture was strong enough to process those influences in an original way. The Iberians had cities surrounded by massive walls made of tremendous chunks of stone. In the cities, which resembled Greek city-states, there were stone houses and paved streets. The Iberian cities maintained a strong influence over the surrounding plains, where people lived on the proceeds of agriculture and animal husbandry. Metalworking, pottery baking, glassblowing, and textile processing were intensively practiced. The apex of this Iberian culture occurred between the fifth and the third centuries BC. From the drawings on vases we have learned that the Iberians decorated their clothing with embroidery and wore sandals and boots. From Greek sources we learn that the Iberians stood out as excellent soldiers. At the same time they were renowned for their talents in music and dancing. Their architecture and sculpture were of a high level and demonstrated their own particular style. In the northern Balkan areas, the culture of the Illyrians paralleled the Hallstatt, while also being strongly influenced by the Greeks and the Romans. East of the Illyrians lived the Thrace people, who were originally influenced by the Hallstatt culture.

The Scythians

The Scythians were often described by the classical writers with a mixture of fear and

The Bloody Funeral Rituals of the Scythians

According to manuscripts written by the Greek author and noted traveler Herodotus, the burial of an important Scythian was accompanied by human sacrifice. The more important the person, the more sacrifices were made at the time of burial.

The funeral rituals were extensive for the Scythians, who apparently believed in an afterlife. The Scythians worshiped animals and totems and displayed great faith in the power of magic, and a number of rituals were performed on behalf of the deceased, often by a shaman, a holy medicine man.

When a king died, lengthy mourning observances were held. A large square hole would be dug as a grave on the banks of the Dnieper River. In preparation for the funeral the body was embalmed with scented herbs. It was then placed on a wagon and gaily paraded around to all the various tribes for a period of forty days. At each tribal site, huge celebrational meals were prepared. During these feasts every participant would cut off his hair, then slice off a piece of his ear and make a cut on his arm, his forehead, and his nose. Finally, he had to pierce his left hand with an arrow.

When the body was finally placed in its grave, one of the deceased's wives, his personal servant, cook, bodyguard, groom, riding horses, and "the firstborn of all animals" were killed and placed in the grave with him.

Numerous burial gifts, such as golden jewelry, golden tableware, special clothes, fur-trimmed carpets, and wall hangings were sent along with him, in order to make his life in the hereafter more pleasant.

On top of the grave, a large burial mound called a *kurgan* was built. The more important the deceased, the higher the mound. Sometimes mounds were over 60 feet (over 18 meters) high. Another huge celebration was held during the funeral itself. Horses, deer, and wild boars were devoured, and beer and wine were drunk in great quantities. There are indications that hennep vapors (hashish) were inhaled as part of the ritual.

A year later the whole mourning process was repeated, and a group of fifty men, previously selected by the king himself, were strangled. Fifty of his best horses were beaten to death. Their bodies were evacuated and stuffed with straw, then sewn closed. With the use of wooden frames, the dead horses were placed upright. The dead men were tied on them in riding position, and they were placed in a circle around the grave.

Such rituals were strictly followed, even for less important people. The forty-day trip to all the relatives was considered particularly important, since the deceased was considered to have retained his predeath powers for that amount of time, but no longer.

admiration. They were known as formidable bareback fighters, particularly talented with bow and arrows. It is possible that the Scythians were the first people to use horses for riding, at around 900 BC. This fact changed their lives significantly: they abandoned their farms, began traveling around as nomads, and probably acquired a taste for conquering and plundering. Once on horseback they tyrannized the people of the Near East and penetrated into Europe as far as the

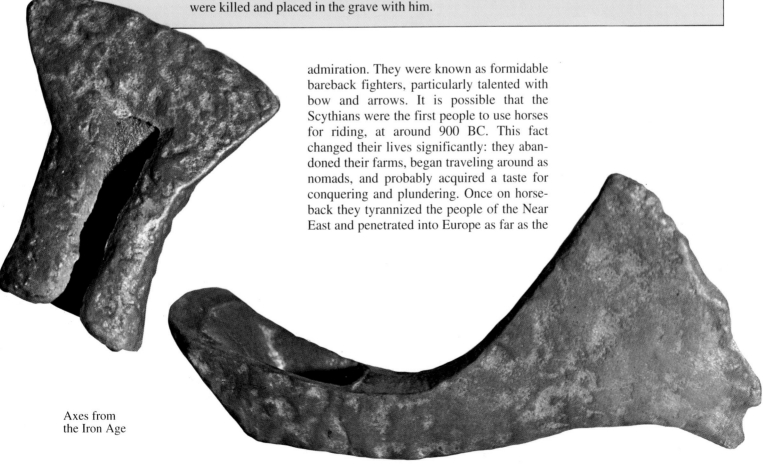

Axes from the Iron Age

Bronze horse bit.
Early Iron Age,
France.

Vistula River in Poland. The wealth of the Scythians lay in a wide zone north of the Black Sea. There we have found *kurgans* (burial mounds), which sometimes comprised entire houses of the dead. The graves of nobility consisted of several rooms in which dead nobles, warriors, slaves, and horses were each separately buried. It is also known that the Scythians beheaded or scalped their prisoners of war and drank from their skulls. It is not surprising, then, that the Greeks shivered when they heard their name. Nonetheless, the Scythians were not completely barbaric. Their harnesses, weapons, jewelry, and clothing bear witness to great artistic talent. Their particular style is characterized by many animal motifs. Among their burial gifts were objects made of bronze, gold, and electrum (an alloy of silver and gold). Not all Scythians lived as nomads. Some continued to work the land. Others lived in settlements that also served as winter quarters for others. They sometimes employed Greek craftspeople. The

122

Celtic bronze ring
with relief decoration.
La Tène culture of Europe.

Romans to subsequently conquer their vast area in a piecemeal fashion. Yet the military talents the Celts arrayed against the Romans were formidable. Armed with swords, lances, and daggers, protected by helmets, shields, and chest harnesses (their smith work was praised by Caesar himself), they reinforced the warlike reputation they held from the Hallstatt period. Their noble class possessed two-wheeled chariots that evidenced great craftsmanship. Their wheels were formed from a single piece of wood and finished with iron; spokes, naves, hubcaps, and mountings were flawless. The clasps and bits of the harnesses gave similar evidence of amazing technical skill.

The aristocratic structure of the Celtic civilization was reinforced in the La Tène period in the first millennium BC. This was a period of Celtic expansion into eastern Europe and the Mediterranean associated with the appearance of La Tène material in

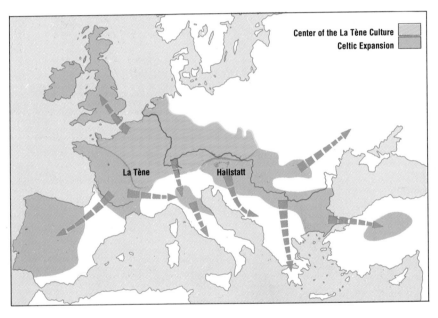

The Celts and Iron Age culture. Arrows represent possible directions of monuments of Celtic groups.

European portion of the Scythian power only disappeared around 300 BC, through the actions of the Celts.

The Invasion of the Celts

The Celts, meanwhile, had not been idle. The knack for expansion that characterized them as far back as the Urnfield and Hallstatt cultures now continued in the subsequent La Tène culture. At about 500 BC they penetrated France, conquered the British Isles, gained a foothold in northern Spain (Galicia) and, across the Alps, spread over northern Italy (Gallia Cisalpina). Nor did they stop at the Po River. They even conquered Rome around 390 BC. (The last Romans were saved, according to legend, only by the honking of the geese of the capital city.) In central Europe, the Gauls (Celts) went into Bohemia, Moravia, Slovakia, and on into southern Poland (Galicia). They appeared in the Balkans, terrorizing the Greeks and establishing themselves in Asia Minor (Galatia). This all took place about 275 BC.

Within two centuries an enormous area had come under Celtic control. The expansion, however, was completely uncoordinated. No Celtic empire ever existed. What occurred were always independent battles initiated by separate groups of people.

It was specifically this loose relationship of the Celts that made it possible for the

these areas at this time. The nobility owned huge plots of land that were worked by serfs, while the owners hunted. The nobles formed bands of warriors with their subordinates as soldiers. These were directed by commanders in chief, who were not otherwise rulers and had little or no power over the nobility. In some bands, in fact, there was no commander: control was put in the hands of a board of elders.

The Celts did not have real urban centers. They did have large settlements that functioned as centers for the outlying farmers and as marketplaces for large areas. Their system of management was too loosely organized for urban centers. The farmers lived in widespread farms or in villages, which were often fortified. Sometimes the fortifications were so extensive, with their heavy walls, ram-

123

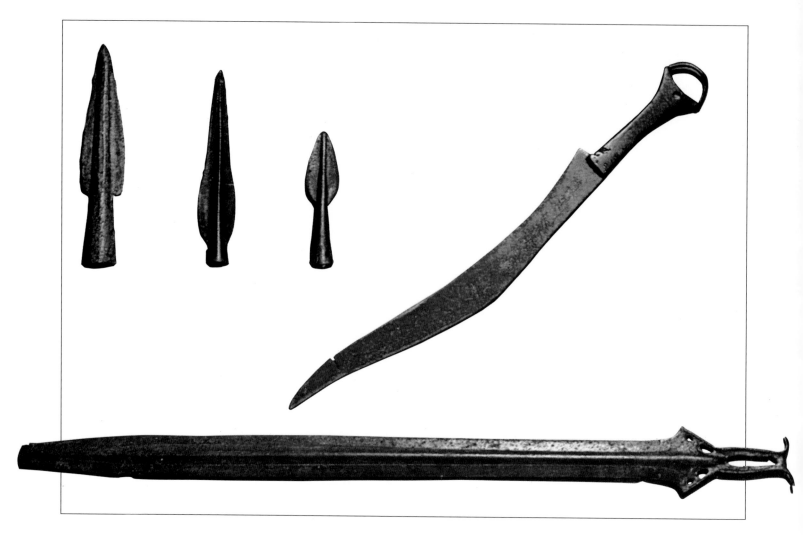

Swords and
lance heads from the
Early Iron Age. Spain.

parts, and canals, that they looked more like fortresses than villages. The Romans repeatedly referred to them as *oppida* (fortress) settlements. The Celtic holy places also had the character of fortresses. These were small, usually square buildings, which must have served as the sites of sacred rituals. Ditches and sacrificial pits have been found at such sites. In the Greek-colonized south of France, they built sanctuaries of stone. Elsewhere, they made these of wood. In one such sanctuary, a consecrated group of statues was surrounded by pillars bearing carved pillars. Niches were carved in these pillars to hold skulls, possibly of conquered people. It is unclear what gods the Celts revered. There were gods of natural forces, of war, of the hunt, and others. Some gods were represented in the form of half-humans or monsters. Roman authors quickly identified them with their own deities. There is believed to have been a pantheon of gods and an extensive trove of Celtic mythological lore. Probably sagas were sung or recited to the nobility by bards, but none of this is certain. The Irish Celtic sources that have reported such details date from a much later time. Only legend surrounds the activities of the Celtic priests or medicine men called Druids.

Celtic sculpture was inspired by the Greeks, but nonetheless shows a powerful style of its own. Its simplicity belies the exuberance of Celtic decorative style. Both

Gold earring
from the Iron Age.
Irixo en Caucos,
Spain.

124

Bronze flagon with ❯
coral and enamel inlay from
Basse Vutz, Lorraine,
France. Celts, fourth century BC.

125

Iron breastplate
from the Hallstatt
culture

Earthenware pot
with characteristic wave
decoration from the
Iron Age

wood and stone were used as material for the images of gods and the masks, statues, and animal figures. Jewelry and functional objects were often totally covered by symmetrical patterns in which stylized illustrations of people and animals with abstract motifs were intertwined. The Celts loved color, as is evidenced by their clothing, and they often decorated metal objects with enamel or pieces of coral or colored glass. Their artistic skills are obvious in their bracelets and rings, sword sheaths, harnesses, wine pitchers, and drinking horns.

The Germanics

Much less is known about the Germanic peoples during the La Tène period than about the Celts. What Caesar and Tacitus have written about them applies to a later time and is not entirely correct. For example, Caesar says that the Celts (Gauls) lived on the western side of the Rhine and the Germanics on the eastern side. But archaeological evidence establishes that southern Germany (on the Rhine's eastern banks) was entirely Celtic at that time. Before the period of expansion the Germanics probably constituted a group of autonomous village communities with no centralized authority or administration. Only in times of war did they choose a manager, a military commander or "ruler." Caesar reports them as having a desire for war and plundering, but there was no sign of it prior to 200 BC. (Perhaps because the population density was so minimal, there was little reason for military expansion then.) The overall evidence of Germanic civilization points to peaceful farmers living in scattered groups. Their lives did not differ much from those of Bronze Age people. Apart from the names of their gods, little is known of their spiritual lives.

Only after 200 BC did the Germanic tribes from the Elbe area begin to organize themselves as warriors and commence their expansion to the south. Historical chronicles reveal the incursions of the Kimbers and Germanics, who went from the Celtic area to Spain and Italy, where they were beaten back by the Roman general Marius around 100 BC. The Elbe Germanics, or Suevi, attacked Celtic France. It was then one of the major goals of the Romans to keep the Germanics, at any cost, on the other side of the Rhine. The Batavians were allies of the Roman authorities and so were permitted, as an exception, to establish themselves along the major rivers. They served quite well as a buffer zone.

With the discussion of the late Iron Age and the arrival of the Romans, we have come to the end of the prehistoric period.

TIME LINE

GEOLOGICAL HISTORY

Years Ago

3.5 billion Formation of the earth

2 billion Primitive plant life evolves on earth

600 million Date of the invertebrates, first fossil remains

400 million Development of vertebrates and fishes

300 million Development of amphibians

248–65 million Mesozoic era

208–144 million Jurassic period of the Mesozoic era

144–65 million Because of continental drift, dinosaurs are not found on every continent

135–65 million Cretaceous period of the Mesozoic era

70–65 million Dinosaurs dominate the earth; mammals begin to diversify by evolution

c.65 million Pleisadapiforme, first–known archaic primate

66 million–present Cenozoic era

56.5–35.5 million Eocene epoch; global warming trend favorable for mammalian evolution; specialized herbivores and carnivore mammals evolve; first–known modern–looking primates evolve (*Adapids* and *Omomydids*), from which all later primates sprang

23.3–5.2 million Miocene epoch; earth's surface evolves into what is essentially its present form; mammalian evolution continues; some of the most successful mammals evolve during this period

5.2–1.6 million Pliocene epoch; large ice sheets form on northern continents, causing ocean levels to drop significantly; hominids begin radiating out of Africa

1.6 million–15,000 Pleistocene epoch; constant fluctuations between warm and intensely cold global climates

Prehistory	Antiquity	Middle Ages	Renaissance	Modern History	Contemporary History

GEOLOGICAL HISTORY	ANTHROPOLOGICAL HISTORY	OTHER WORLD EVENTS

40–30 million Oligopithecids and Parapithecids; first mammal with characteristics of anthropoid primates, though no known descendants exist

35–30 million Evolution of Propliopithecids, among which is *Aegypyopithecus*, fossil evidence found in Fayum Depression of Egypt; Propliopithecids possess distinctly anthropoid features, like those of modern monkeys, such as limbs for leaping and climbing and forward–facing eye sockets

30 million Dryopithecus

23–14 million Proconsul, likely ancestor of both apes and monkeys of the Old World, including chimps, gorillas, and apes

15 million Kenyapithecus, derived from Proconsul, close common ancestor of later large hominoids

3.5–2.6 million *Australopithecus afarensis;* the oldest species of Australopithecus; fossil remains found in East Africa at Hadar (Ethiopia), Koobi Fora (Kenya), and Laetoli (Tanzania); "Lucy"; habitually bipedal with dexterous hands for grasping and small brains; Homo lineage probably an offshoot of *A. afarensis*

3–2 million *Australopithecus africanus;* fossil remains found in South Africa at Taung, Sterkfontain, and Makapansgat; resembles *A. afarensis* in bipedalism and hand form, though the face of *A. africanus* was proportionately larger

2.8–2.2 million *Australopithecus aethiopicus;* fossil remains found at Omo (Ethiopia) and West Turkana (Kenya)

2.0–1.0 million *Australopithecus robustus;* fossil evidence recovered in South Africa at Swartkrans and Kromdraai; existed larger than *A. africanus*; though also capable of bipedalism, this species is only a distant cousin to human ancestors

2.5–1.5 million Oldowan, oldest stone tools
2.5 million–200,000 Lower Paleolithic Age; divided into two phases of hominid and technological evolution: Oldowan and Acheulean

2.4–1.8 million "Early Homo" (*Homo habilis* and *Homo rudolphensis);* first tool–producing human ancestor; fossil remains found in East Africa at Koobi Fora, Kenya

1.8 million–1.6 million *Homo erectus* remains found in both Africa and Southeast Asia
1.8 million–75,000 *Homo erectus*; larger bodies and brains than "Early Homo" forebears; fossil remains from Africa, China, and Java; possibly the first human ancestor to migrate out of Africa; migrations probably occurred rapidly and coincided with the migrations of animals across the continents

1.5 million–200,000 Acheulean, stone tool culture that follows Oldowan

700,000 Archaic *Homo sapiens,* also known as Neandertal; this species of early human is distinguished from *Homo erectus* by its larger brain; survived until about 35,000 years ago in Western Europe
700,000 Ubeidiya, Israel; earliest recordedhuman settle-ment in the Near East; probably *Homo erectus*

Prehistory	Antiquity	Middle Ages	Renaissance	Modern History	Contemporary History

GEOLOGICAL HISTORY	ANTHROPOLOGICAL HISTORY	OTHER WORLD EVENTS

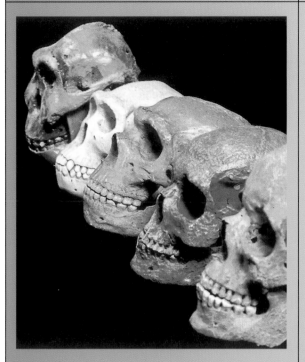

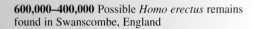

600,000–400,000 Possible *Homo erectus* remains found in Swanscombe, England

400,000 Earliest evidence for controlled use of fire

c.300,000 *Homo erectus* is replaced by archaic *Homo sapiens* in Africa; *H. erectus* continues to survive in East Asia until 75,000 years ago

200,000 *Homo sapiens sapiens,* Anatomically Modern Human, gradually expands from Africa to parts of Asia and the Near East
200,000 In Eurasia the Mousterian culture replaces the Acheulean

100,000 The Levallois technique of stone tool production is developed
100,000–32,000 Archaic *Homo sapiens;* Neandertal remains found in Africa, the Near East, and Europe
100,000–30,000 The Mousterian culture (generally associated with Neandertals) flourishes in Europe and the Near East; more specialized tools are made; verbal communication through language may have developed during this time

90,000 Anatomically Modern Humans (AMH), *Homo sapiens sapiens,* occupy Qafzeh cave, Israel, probably coexisting with Neandertals at this time in the Near East

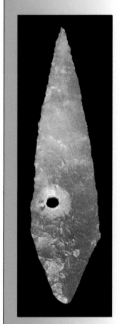

40,000–32,000 *Homo sapiens sapiens* spread into Europe with more sophisticated technologies and cognitive abilities than Neandertals; the first Anatomically Modern Humans to occupy Europe are often referred to as Cro–Magnon people; AMH eventually replaced Neandertals.

35,000–32,000 Middle–Upper Paleolithic transition in Eurasia; dramatic cultural change occurs in social organization, technological sophistication, and artistic representation; Neandertals cease to exist during this time

35,000–28,000 Earliest art in human and animal figurines

32,000 Most recent date of Neandertal remains found in Europe, after which time all skeletal remains are those of AMH, *Homo sapiens sapiens*

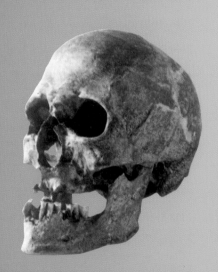

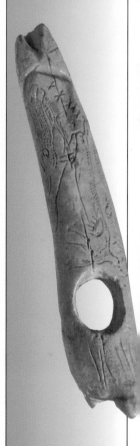

20,000–18,000 Pleistocene glaciers are at the peak of their territorial reach; sea levels are much lower and temperatures colder than the present day

18,000–11,000 Global climate gradually gets warmer; glaciers retreat to northern latitudes; sea levels rise; flora and fauna undergo dramatic changes

16,000–11,000 Magdalenian tradition across Europe reaches height in cave and rock art, carvings of wild animals, decorated weapons

13,000 Earliest radiocarbon–dated evidence for occupation of the New World found at Monte Verde, Chile

12,500–10, 500 Natufian culture of the Levant flourishes

c.10,000 Neolithic revolution in the Near East; domestication of plants and animals, increased sedentary lifestyle, and social complexity

Prehistory	Antiquity	Middle Ages	Renaissance	Modern History	Contemporary History

	GEOLOGICAL HISTORY	ANTHROPOLOGICAL HISTORY	OTHER WORLD EVENTS
BC			
7000		**c.7000** Farming takes hold in Greece and Southeast Europe; European Mesolithic culture	
6000		**c.6000–4000** Development of metallurgy technology; increasingly widespread use of copper and bronze in the Near East	**6000** Earliest maize cultivation in Mesoamerica
		6000–3500 Farming spreads into western Europe; copperworking and megaliths become benchmarks of European culture of this time	
5000		**5300** Linear bandkeramik complex, best–known farming culture of Europe, first occupies Central Europe and spreads as far west as Holland	
4000		**c.4000–3000** Urban revolution in the Near East	
3000		**c.3000** Invention of writing in Mesopotamia	
		c.2600 The plow is introduced into European farming economy, changing settlement patterns and social organizations; bell–shaped beakers found as artifacts in graves and burial mounds are widespread over Europe from this time up to 2000 BC	**2650** First pyramid erected in Egypt by Pharaoh Djoser
2500		**2500–2000** Chariot introduced, probably from Ural Mountains, heightening the movement of people, ideas, and technologies across Asia and Europe	**c.2500** Phoenicians reach the east coast of the Mediterranean Sea
			2340–2200 Akkadian Empire in Mesopotamia
			2040–1640 Middle Empire in Egypt
2000		**2000–1300** Metallurgy becomes widespread in Europe	**2000** Beginning of the Preclassical Maya period
			1900–1200 Palace period on Crete and Mycenae
		1300–1000 Urnfield culture, so called because ashes of cremated dead deposited in urns, dominates Europe; age of skilled warriors and metalsmiths	**1792–1750** Codex Hammurabi in Mesopotamia
			1600 Plundering of Babylon by the Hittites
1500			**c.1500** Flourishing of the Hittite Empire
			1478 Hatshepsut reigns as pharaoh over Egypt
			1450 Development of Linear B on Mycenae
			1350 Erecting of the Lions Gate on Mycenae
			1300 Bronze production invented independently in China by Shang culture
			1300 Olmec civilization on the Caribbean coast
			1286 Battle at Kadesj
			1224 Exodus of the Israeli people from Egypt
			c.1200 *Rig Veda* in India
			1200–1000 Doric invasions in Greece; end of the Mycenaean civilization
			1050–750 Dark Ages in Greece
			1027 Zhou dynasty in China
			1000–966 David king of the Israeli people
1000		**1000** Use and production of iron spreads quickly across Europe	**753** Legendary foundation of Rome
			750–700 Homer's *Iliad* and *Odyssey*

Prehistory	Antiquity	Middle Ages	Renaissance	Modern History	Contemporary History

	GEOLOGICAL HISTORY	ANTHROPOLOGICAL HISTORY	OTHER WORLD EVENTS
BC 700		**700-600** Hallstatt culture spreads over Urnfield territory, to dominate much of Central and Eastern Europe	
600			**660** Legendary foundation of the state of Japan
			586 Babylonian captivity of the Jewish people
			580–504 Pythagoras argues that the earth is round; geocentrism, the sun rotates around the earth
			521–486 Darius I king of the Persians
			509 Beginning of the Roman Republic
500		**c.500** Scythians emerge as powerful warriors from Eastern Europe **c.500-250** Expansion of the Celts	**500** Greece founds colonies in Sicily and southern Italy
			478/7 Foundation of the Attic–Delian Union
			c.390 Celts sack Rome
250			**260–200** Apollonius introduces the theory of the epicycle to explain the orbits of planets
AD 150			**c.150** Ptolemaeus sets in order all known facts about the earth and the universe
1000			**1054** Supernova, explosion of stars
			1473–1543 Copernicus's heliocentric philosophy, the sun as the center of the solar system
1500			
1600			**c.1600** Invention of the telescope by Christiaan Huygens
			1609 Galileo Galilei is first to use the telescope
			1643–1727 Gravitation theory of Isaac Newton, discovery of the spectrum
1700			**1735** Linnaeus's *Systema Naturae*
			1769–1832 Cuvier's *Discours sur les revolutions de la surface du globe*
			1789 Herschel's reflector
1800			**c.1800** Black lines are discovered in the spectrum of the sun **c.1800–1850** Remains of extinct plants and animals are found
			c.1825 Invention of photography and spectroscopy
1850			**c.1850** Formulation of geological time scale
			1856 Finding of an incomplete skeleton of a Neandertal near Düsseldorf
1860			**1859** Charles Darwin's *On the Origin of Species*
1870			**1868** E. Lartet discovers five human skeletons in the Cro–Magnon area
1880			**1886** Fossil remains of the Neandertaler found near Namen

Prehistory	Antiquity	Middle Ages	Renaissance	Modern History	Contemporary History

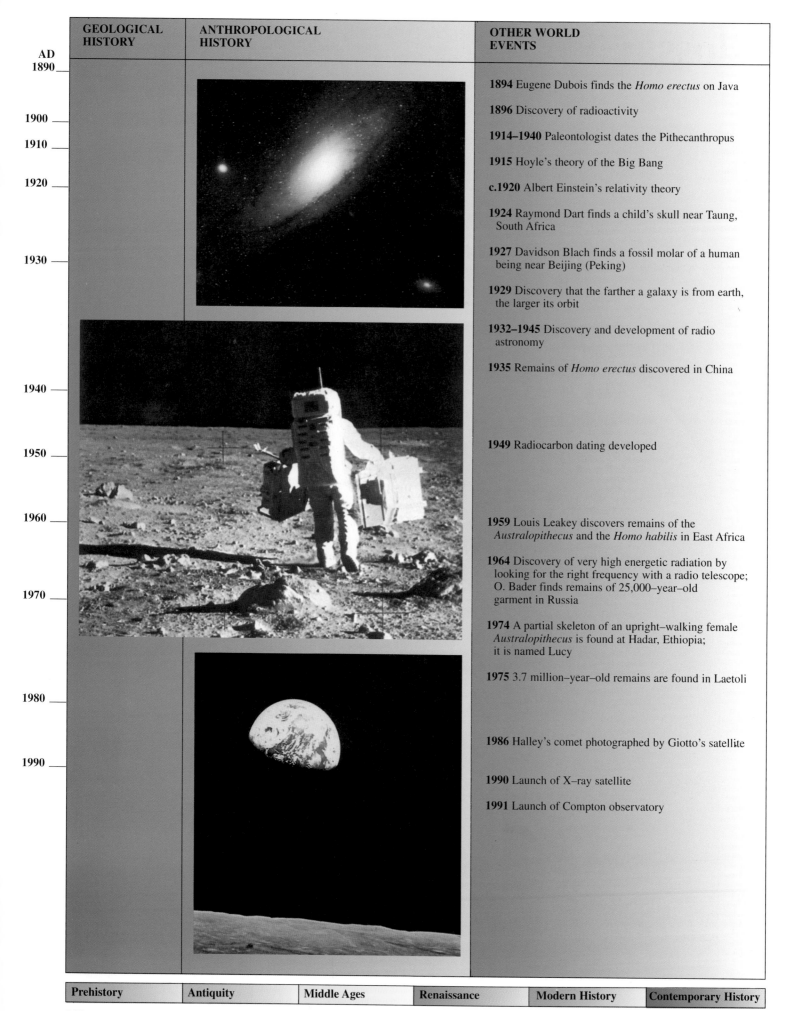

GEOLOGICAL HISTORY	ANTHROPOLOGICAL HISTORY		OTHER WORLD EVENTS

AD
1890

1900

1910

1920

1930

1940

1950

1960

1970

1980

1990

1894 Eugene Dubois finds the *Homo erectus* on Java

1896 Discovery of radioactivity

1914–1940 Paleontologist dates the Pithecanthropus

1915 Hoyle's theory of the Big Bang

c.1920 Albert Einstein's relativity theory

1924 Raymond Dart finds a child's skull near Taung, South Africa

1927 Davidson Blach finds a fossil molar of a human being near Beijing (Peking)

1929 Discovery that the farther a galaxy is from earth, the larger its orbit

1932–1945 Discovery and development of radio astronomy

1935 Remains of *Homo erectus* discovered in China

1949 Radiocarbon dating developed

1959 Louis Leakey discovers remains of the *Australopithecus* and the *Homo habilis* in East Africa

1964 Discovery of very high energetic radiation by looking for the right frequency with a radio telescope; O. Bader finds remains of 25,000–year–old garment in Russia

1974 A partial skeleton of an upright–walking female *Australopithecus* is found at Hadar, Ethiopia; it is named Lucy

1975 3.7 million–year–old remains are found in Laetoli

1986 Halley's comet photographed by Giotto's satellite

1990 Launch of X–ray satellite

1991 Launch of Compton observatory

Prehistory	Antiquity	Middle Ages	Renaissance	Modern History	Contemporary History

Glossary

Abbevillian culture offshoot of Acheulean Paleolithic culture from 400,000 years ago, named for the northern African town, Abbeville, near which remnants were discovered.

Acheulean a stone tool-making tradition that developed around 1.5 million years ago in East Africa. The Acheulean tradition replaced the preceding Oldowan tradition, with its use of stone tools. This cultural change closely corresponds to the biological transition from "early *Homo*"to *Homo erectus*.

alignments megaliths or prehistoric stone monuments placed in long rows.

Anatomically Modern Humans (AMH) *Homo sapiens sapiens;* present-day humans, once known as Cro-Magnon.

artifact any object once made or used by humans and recovered archaeologically.

asteroid belt orbit of asteroids between Mars and Jupiter.

Australopithecus upright-walking hominid from 4 million years ago, found in Africa.

bandkeramik Neolithic culture of northern and central Europe dating from 5000 BC, recognized by its pottery decorations of distinct linear patterning.

Bell-beaker culture a group of Neolithic cultures between 2600 and 2000 BC that spread from Spain to northern Africa and over western and central Europe. It is named after its characteristic ceramic forms. These people are thought to have been the first in western Europe to process metals, particularly copper.

Big Bang theory postulates the creation of the universe from the explosion of a quantity of very dense material and energy that formed atoms and thus the eventual universe.

black hole region in the universe with such a strong field of gravity that nothing can escape, created out of very heavy stars whose nuclei have collapsed during a supernova explosion.

bronze copper-tin alloy widely used by 1700 BC.

Bronze Age period during which bronze became the most important basic material, varying from culture to culture; began about 5500 BC in the Near East and 3000 BC in Europe.

C14 method a dating method based upon the radioactivity of the C14 isotope of carbon.

cave paintings found throughout prehistory; especially noteworthy are hundreds of Paleolithic European examples.

Celts name given to a group of people occupying central and western Europe, from the British Isles to Hungary, from 1000 BC. Bearers of the Celtic civilization are the Hallstatt culture and the La Tène culture, which share stylistic continuities. The Urnfield culture also shows Celtic characteristics.

Cenozoic age 66 million years ago to the present.

clusters groups comprising dozens to thousands of galaxies held together through their mutual gravity. The Milky Way, the Magellanic Clouds, and the Andromeda nebula constitute a part of the local group. Clusters are grouped into superclusters.

comet nebulous celestial body of small mass revolving around the Sun, composed of a relatively dense tenacious mass of dust, gas, or a mixture of each; often develops a tail when traveling in the part of its orbit nearest the Sun.

Copernicus, Nicolaus (1473–1543) Polish astronomer who first conceived of a *heliocentric* (sun-centered) solar system.

copper reddish brown metallic element.

corpse silhouette light discoloration in the ground left by a decomposed skeleton.

Cretaceous period in the Mesozoic age, from 144 to 66 million years ago.

Cro-Magnon outdated term for *Homo sapiens sapiens*, or modern human livings some 200,000 years ago.

cromlechs See henge monuments.

Cryptozoic age in Earth history from 2 billion to 600 million years ago.

Darwin, Charles (1809–1882) English naturalist who postulated the theory of evolution.

delta-cepheids pulsating stars that vary in surface temperature, color, and light intensity as they change size, alternately becoming smaller and larger.

dendrochronology dating method based on the comparison of annual rings of trees.

dinosaurs reptiles in the Mesozoic age that lived on land and walked upright.

Doppler effect (red shift) change of wavelength frequency of objects by virtue of their relative distance from Earth. The same effect also occurs with sound (for example, a siren coming closer). Because space expands (constellations that are farther away move away from us faster than those nearer to us), this phenomenon can be used to measure distance.

drag plow the oldest type of plow used for tilling land; an important technical innovation in agriculture; probably in general use about 2500 BC.

Dryopithecus tree ape living during the Miocene era (30 million years ago). There was an evolutionary relationship between this ape and later anthropod species, including hominid.

earthenware vessels and containers made of baked clay, in widespread use for cooking and storage by Neolithic cultures.

Einstein, Albert (1879–1955) German-American physicist who developed the theory of relativity.

epicycle theory obsolete theory that explained the geocentric conception of our solar system. It stated that a planet revolves in a circle (epicycle) around a central point, which moves in a large circle around the Earth.

extragalactic systems galaxies outside the Milky Way, visible from the Earth as nebulae of gas.

fauna term adopted by Linnaeus in 1746 to designate animals of a specifed region or time; often used with flora (plants).

Flamsteed, Sir John (1646–1719) first Royal Astronomer of England.

flint hard type of stone in calcium and chalk layers, easily chipped to make tools; widely used in the Paleolithic and Mesolithic ages.

flora term adopted by Linnaeus in 1745 to designate plants of a specified region or time.

fossils hardened remains or imprints of plants and animals, particularly skeletons or shells, preserved in layers of rock.

Funnel-beaker culture Neolithic culture around 2500 BC in northern and central Europe, named for the shape of their characteristic earthenware.

Fraunhofer, Joseph von (1787–1826) Bavarian optician and physicist, investigated spectra of planets and invented light-measuring instruments and ways to improve telescopes.

geocentric concept of the world Earth-centered concept of the solar system, prevailing from antiquity until the sixteenth century AD.

geologic timescale timescale with which the developments of the Earth's crust are dated. By studying sedimentary and igneous rocks, relative dates can be established. By determining the half-lives of radioactive elements in minerals, geologic periods can be absolutely dated.

Germanics people in northwestern Europe who migrated southward, beginning around 200 BC.

gulf streams great currents of warm water in the ocean that affect the temperature of both the surrounding seas and the air above them.

Hallstatt culture central European culture of the late Bronze and early Iron Ages, from 1200–475 BC.

hand-axe a Paleolithic tool originally made of flint; increasingly made of other stones, it was refined through the Paleolithic age.

heliocentric concept of the world concept of the solar system as sun-centered, with the planets revolving around the Sun; first postulated by Copernicus in 1543.

henge monuments circles of megaliths or stone monuments (such as Stonehenge in England) whose purposes and origins are as yet unknown.

Hittites people who established an empire around 2000 BC in Asia Minor and were the first to base their power on iron processing. The apex of their civilization was around 1500 BC. Their empire disappeared around 1200 BC.

Holocene era in the Quaternary period beginning 10,000 years ago, during which the temperature and the sea level rose; can be viewed as an interglacial period of the Pleistocene age that is still continuing.

hominids a class of primates that includes *Homo habilis, Homo erectus, Homo sapiens,* and all *Australopithecus* species. This group also includes all the great apes, including humans, gorillas, orangutans, and chimpanzees.

Homo erectus hominid who walked upright and lived from 150,000 to 500,000 years ago in Africa, Asia, and Europe; the first hominid species to be found outside Africa; includes Java man (*Pithecanthropus*) and Peking man; used tools, made shelters, and utilized fires.

Homo habilis hominid who walked upright; lived some 2 million years ago, at the same time as *Australopithecus*; first hominid species found in association with manufactured tools.

Homo sapiens sapiens modern man; developed around 200,000 years ago; displaced Neandertals around 30,000 years ago.

Iberian culture non-Celtic Iron Age culture in Spain and southern France. High point of this culture was from the fifth to the third centuries BC. The Iberians survived on agriculture and animal husbandry.

ice ages (glacials) climatic episodes characterized by a great drop in temperature, the expansion of ice caps at regions of higher latitude (such as North America and northern and central Europe), and changes in flora and fauna. Between about 600,000 and 10,000 years ago there were four primary cold

waves, corresponding to the cultures of the Paleolithic age.

immersion technique boiling water by dropping red-hot stones into it; used since Paleolithic times.

Indo-European a common-language family of European and a few Asiatic (Indian) languages.

inner planets planets with an orbit between Earth and the Sun, specifically Mercury and Venus.

interglacials episodes between the ice ages that were characterized by a mild subtropical climate, an elevated sea level, and consequent changes in flora and fauna.

interpluvials periods between pluvials. See pluvials.

interstellar material material consisting of gas and dust in the space between the stars.

iron metal that is obtained by heating iron ore and hammering it for a long period of time, after which it is shaped into objects. Iron was already being processed in western Asia in 2000 BC by Armenian tribes. It is more readily available and produced more easily than bronze.

Iron Age period after the Bronze Age during which the major weapons and tools were made of iron. The Hittites formed the first Iron Age culture, about 1500 BC. Between 1200 and 600 BC, ironworking spread over Europe and Asia.

Jurassic period in the Mesozoic from 208 to 144 million years ago, named after the Jura Mountains. During this period, flying reptiles and early ancestral birds evolved.

Kepler, Johannes (1571–1630) German astronomer who defended Copernicus's teachings. He wrote the laws of Kepler that account for the movement of the planets.

Kirchhoff, Gustav Robert (1824–1887) German physicist.

kitchen waste mounds huge garbage piles, mainly of mollusk shells, left by a Mesolithic culture on the North Sea and Atlantic coasts.

kurgans large burial mounds of the Scythians, used for kings and high officials.

La Tène culture Celtic Iron Age culture (475–40 BC).

Levallois technique a planned method of flint processing. Flakes struck from the original core of flint are worked into tools with precise retouching blows.

linear bandkeramik *See bandkeramik.*

Linnaeus, Carolus (1707–1778) Swedish botanist who developed the system for classifying plants and animals by genus (always capitalized) and species.

Lower Paleolithic period from about 1.5 million to 180,000 years ago.

Magdalenian culture in Europe in the Upper Paleolithic between about 15,000 and 9000 BC, the end of the last ice age. The Magdalenian people mainly hunted reindeer, which were plentiful during this episode of the last Ice Age. They produced tools of bone and antler, rather than those exclusively of flint.

Magellanic Clouds star systems that accompany the Milky Way galaxy, divided into the Large and the Small Magellanic Clouds; irregular in shape.

mammals vertebrate warm-blooded animals, with skin more or less covered with hair, that dominated the Cenozoic age, evolved from mammallike predecessors in the Mesozoic age. Mammals normally bear and nurse live young, but egg-laying mammals also exist.

mammoth large woolly elephants with enormous tusks who lived in tundra areas during the cold periods of the Pleistocene era. They died out around 8000 BC.

megaliths large prehistoric stone monuments. *See* alignments, henge monuments. and menhirs.

menhirs pillarlike stone monuments or megaliths that apparently served as sacrificial sites.

Mesolithic period from about 10,000 to 8000 BC, characterized by a warmer climate and a greater specialization in hunting by people who lived in semipermanent base camps. The age gradually ended as agriculture was introduced.

Mesozoic period from about 248 to 66 million years ago. It is subdivided into the Triassic, Jurassic, and Cretaceous periods. During the Mesozoic age, Earth was dominated by dinosaurs. In addition, birdlike creatures and mammallike species developed.

meteor meteoroid that leaves a visible white trail as it hits Earth's atmosphere; a shooting star.

meteorite mass of metal or stone that has fallen on Earth or other planets from space.

meteoroid solid body traveling through outer space.

Middle Paleolithic period from 180,000 to 34,000 years ago; its distinction is based on lithic technology. The range of tools was expanded and refined with the Levallois technique. The culture of the period is called the Mousterian, and tools from this period have been discovered with Neandertal remains.

Milky Way galaxy star system of which our solar system is a part; in appearance, a flat disk with a spiral structure consisting of thin gas and hundreds of billions of stars.

moons celestial bodies orbiting planets through gravitational attraction.

moraines an accumulation of earth and stone that once formed at the edges and undersides of glaciers and was deposited after the ice melted.

Mousterian Middle Paleolithic cultural period in Europe from 200,000 to 70,000 years ago.

Natufian Mesolithic culture in the Near East; people lived by hunting, fishing, and the gathering of wild grains, which were processed with harvesting equipment and millstones.

Neandertal archaic branch of *Homo sapiens* classified today as *Homo sapiens Neandertalensis;* lived between 75,000 and 30,000 years ago in Europe and Asia, during the Mousterian culture.

Neolithic period from 8000 to 2000 BC, characterized by a shift from hunting to agriculture, animal husbandry, and permanent settlements.

Neolithic revolution the gradual transition from hunting and gathering to domestication of plants and animals.

neutron stars formed from neutral particles of atoms; collapsed nuclei of atoms, with a strong magnetic field; those visible on Earth are called pulsars, because their rapid rotation can be seen as pulsating X rays.

Newton, Isaac (1642–1727) English mathematician, physicist, and astronomer. He postulated theories on the relationship between mass, velocity, and energy and studied the composition of sunlight.

nova heavy star that explodes at the end of its life, collapsing into a neutron star or a black hole. Supernovas are very large novas.

Oligopithecus after the Greek *oligos* (small) and *pithekos* (ape); important findings of small ape fossils found in the Fayum Depression in Egypt.

outer planets planets with an orbit outside Earth's, specifically Mars, Jupiter, Saturn, Uranus, Neptune, and Pluto.

Paleozoic period from about 600 million to 248 million years ago, subdivided into various periods. Characterized by the evolution of vertebrate animals, including amphibians, the first animals to live on land.

Peking man (*Sinanthropus pekinensis*) hominid belonging to *Homo erectus,* discovered in China in the 1930s by Franz Weidenreich, Pierre Teilhard de Chardin, and others. This hominid species were hunters and used fire; lived some 400,000 to 200,000 years ago.

Pithecanthropus erectus upright anthropoid whose thighbone and crown were reported to be the missing link between ape and man; discovered in Java in 1891 by Eugene Dubois.

planet any celestial body revolving around a star.

planetesimals small heavenly bodies created from the coalescence of dust particles remaining after star formation; planets are formed through their collision.

planetoids planetesimals that have not formed into planets.

Pleistocene era in the Quaternary during which the ice ages occurred; dated from 1.8 million to 10,000 years ago.

pluvials climate changes in northern Africa and the Middle East characterized by greater quantities of precipitation. These are associated with the growth of ice caps on the northern hemisphere during the ice ages. The periods between pluvials are called interpluvials.

pollen method dating method based upon the identification of pollen grains; plant species correspond to specific climatic changes.

prehistory period of human history before the development of writing; knowledge of this time is based on archaeological sources and scientific dating methods.

primate any member of the most highly developed order of mammals, including humans, apes, monkeys, and lemurs.

prosimians half-apes that developed strongly over the Oligocene epoch (about 40 million years ago).

protohistory period in the history of humans that lies between prehistory and history; knowledge of this period is based upon archaeological materials and the few historical resources left by other peoples who already used writing.

Protruding-foot beaker culture (single-grave culture) Neolithic culture around 2500 BC in northern Europe, named after its typical earthenware forms.

quasar (quasi-stellar object) a name for galaxies located far away that, viewed from the surface, look like stars and have a bright nucleus.

Quaternary period in the Cenozoic from about 1.5 million years ago to the present.

radio-astronomy study of the radio rays of celestial bodies.

satellite anything, man-made or natural, that is in orbit around a central body, including Earth.

Scythians western Asian and Russian herdsmen from the eighth century BC, north of the Black Sea; nomadic horsemen, they plundered the Near East and eastern Europe.

smiths specialized metalworkers.

solar system any system of a central star with celestial bodies in orbit around it.

spectral analysis analysis of the electromagnetic radiation of heavenly bodies through which one can determine their chemical compositions, movements, and temperatures; temperature also gives an indication of such factors as the size and longevity of stars, which are therefore classified on the basis of their spectra.

spectroscopy study of the spectra of starlight.

spectrum a band of colors ranging from red through orange, yellow, green, blue, and indigo to violet, created by the passage of white light through a prism, a rainbow is a visible spectrum; not all spectra can be seen.

speed of light speed with which a light particle travels through a vacuum; is also the greatest speed with which a signal can travel.

star gaseous heavenly body consisting mostly of hydrogen and helium, which emits energy caused by internal nuclear fusion processes; universe consists of huge numbers of stars, the nearest of which is the Sun.

Sun star in the Milky Way galaxy and central point of our solar system. It was born 4.6 billion years ago and will expand, over a period of 6 billion more years, to become a red giant star. After that it will gradually blow off its outer layers, become a white dwarf star, and go out.

tell artificial mound made up of the waste layers and ruins of older cultures, upon which new cultures were established.

terps mounds primarily consisting of kitchen waste and earth, dating from 400 BC, particularly in low coastal areas along the North Sea. They provide useful evidence of human occupation.

Tertiary period in the Cenozoic from about 66 to 1.5 million years ago, divided into the Paleocene, Eocene, Oligocene, Miocene, and Pliocene eras when mammals and hominids developed.

trepanation prehistoric surgery to remove a piece of skull.

Triassic period in the Mesozoic from 248 to 208 million years ago, characterized by the development of reptiles into a wide range of dinosaur species.

tribal houses Neolithic structures housing several families.

tumuli Neolithic burial mounds of the Protruding-foot beaker culture and the Funnel-beaker cultures.

universe approximately 15 billion years old; continues to expand.

135

Upper Paleolithic period from 34,000 to 10,000 BC, characterized by technical innovations in lithic processing and symbolic representation; tools became increasingly specialized; four overlapping cultural periods within this era are identified as the Aurignacian, the Gravettian, the Solutrean, and the Magdalenian.

Urnfield culture late Bronze Age culture between 1600 and 800 BC found throughout central Europe in which the ashes of the cremated deceased were buried in urns.

Bibliography

The Universe

Audouze, J. *The Cambridge Atlas of Astronomy.* Cambridge, 1985.

Gingerich, O. *The Eye of Heaven.* New York, 1993.

Kovalesky, J. *Modern Astronomy.* Berlin, 1995.

Krauss, J. D. *Radio Astronomy.* Powell, OH, 1986.

Mitton, J. *A Concise Dictionary of Astronomy.* Oxford, 1991.

Mitton, S. and Mitton, J. *Astronomy.* Oxford, 1994.

Newton, J. *The guide to Amateur Astronomy.* Cambridge, 1988.

O'Meara, D. J. *Pythagoras Revived.* Oxford, 1989.

Pasachoff, J. M. *Astronomy.* Philadelphia, 1987.

Zombeck, M. V. *Handbook of Space Astronomy and Astrophysics.* Cambridge, 1994.

The Universe Today

Hayashi, C. *Origin of the Solar System.* Kyoto, 1988.

Jones, B. W. *The Solar System.* Oxford, 1984.

Macfarlane, I. *The Black Hole.* London, 1975.

Meadows, J. *Space Garbage.* London, 1985.

———. *Guest Star.* London, 1985.

Sharov, A. *Edwin Hubble, the Discoverer of the Big Bang Universe.* Cambridge, 1993.

Siwel, L. *The Magic of Physics.* Basingstoke, 1987.

Thomas, W.A. *The Big Bang.* Oxford, 1986.

Our Place in the Universe

Browne, J. *Charles Darwin: a Biography.* London, 1995.

Colbert, E. H. *The Dinosaur Book.* New York, 1945.

Denett, D. C. *Darwin's Dangerous Idea.* New York, 1995.

Emiliani, C. *Planet Earth.* Cambridge, 1992.

Erwin, D. H. *The Great Paleozoic Crisis.* Columbia, 1993.

Wilford, J. N. *The Riddle of the Dinosaur.* London, 1986.

Human Evolution

Andersen, B. C. *The Ice Age World.* Oslo, 1994.

Bendall, D.S., ed. *Evolution from Molecules to Man.* Cambridge, 1980.

Gooch, S. *The Neanderthal Question.* London, 1977.

Juritzky, A. *Prehistoric Man as an Artist.* Amsterdam, 1953.

Knight, C. R. *Prehistoric Man: the Great Adventurer.* New York, 1949.

Matthews, J., ed. *Man's Place in Evolution.* Cambridge, 1980.

Nilssen, T. *The Pleistocene.* London, 1983.

Sutcliffe, A. J. *On the Track of Ice Age Mammals.* London, 1985.

The Paleolithic Period

Bordes, F. *The Old Stone Age.* London, 1968.

Clark, G. *The Stone Age Hunters.* London, 1967.

Davis, D. M. *Journey into the Stone Age.* London, 1969.

Osborn, J. R. *Stone Age to Iron Age.* London, 1978.

Quennel, M. *Everyday Life in the Old Stone Age.* London, 1955.

Sahlins, M. *Stone Age Economics.* London, 1974.

Wymer, J. *The Paleolithic Age.* London, 1982.

The Mesolithic and Neolithic Periods

Bender, B. *Farming in Prehistory.* London, 1975.

Clark, G. *World Prehistory in New Perspective.* Cambridge, 1977.

Cunliffe, B., ed. *Oxford Illustrated Prehistory of Europe.* Oxford, 1994.

Gebauer, A.B., ed. *Transitions to Agriculture in Prehistory.* Madison, WI, 1992.

Mellars, P., ed. *Emergence of Modern Humans.* Edinburgh, 1990.

Price, T. D., ed. *Prehistoric Hunter-Gatherers.* Orlando, 1984.

Rindos, D. *The Origins of Agriculture.* New York, 1983.

Szelag, Tadeusz. *New Stone Age Archaeology.* Warsaw, 1987.

Wenke, R. J. *Patterns in Prehistory.* New York, 1990.

The Neolithic Period

Bradley, R. J., ed. *Neolithic Studies.* Oxford, 1984.

Burgess, C. *The Age of Stonehenge.* London, 1980.

Cole, S. *The Neolithic Revolution.* London, 1970.

Hodder, I. *The Domestication of Europe.* Oxford, 1990.

Quennel, M. *Everyday Life in the New Stone, Bronze and Early Iron Ages.* London, 1955.

Whittle, A. W. R. *Neolithic Europe.* Cambridge, 1985.

Prehistoric Humans

Barker, G. *Prehistoric Farming in Europe.* Cambridge, 1985.

Brumfield, E. M., et al. *Specialisation, Exchange and Complex Societies.* Cambridge, 1987.

Croes, D. R. et al. *Long-Term Subsistence Change in Prehistoric North America.* Greenwich, CT, 1992.

Jochim, M. A. *Hunter-Gatherer Subsistence and Settlement.* New York, 1976.

Killion, T. W. *Gardens of Prehistory.* Alabama, 1992.

Lemonier, P. *Technological Choices.* London, 1993.

Wheeler, M. *Civilisations of the Indus Valley and Beyond.* London, 1966.

The Bronze Age

Burgess, C. *Bronze Age Hoards.* Oxford, 1979.

Coles, J.M., and Harding, A.F. *The Bronze Age in Europe.* London, 1979.

Immerwahr, S. A. *The Neolithic and Bronze Ages.* Princeton, 1971.

Thompson, T. L. *The Settlement of Palestine in the Bronze Age*. Wiesbaden, 1979.

Developing Use of Metals
Adouze, F. *Towns, Villages and Countryside of Celtic Europe*. London, 1992.
Collis, J. *Oppida*. Sheffield, 1984.
———. *The European Iron Age*. London, 1984.
Finlay, I. *Celtic Art: An Introduction*. London, 1973.
Hedeager, L. *Iron-Age Societies*. Oxford, 1992.
Powell, T.G.E. *The Celts*. London, 1980.
Rankin, H.D. *Celts and the Classical World*. London, 1987.

The Iron Age
Goffart, W. *Barbarians and Romans*. Princeton, 1980.
Gurney, O. R. *The Hittites*. Harmondsworth, 1980.
Hoffner, H. A. *Hittite Myth*. Atlanta, 1990.
Piotrovsky, B., et al. *Scythian Art*. Oxford, 1987.
Todd, M. *The Northern Barbarians*. London, 1975.
———. *The Early Germans*. Oxford, 1992

Further Reading

Anderson, M. J. *Charles Darwin: Naturalist*. Springfield, NJ, 1987.

Asimov, I. *How Did We Find Out About Comets?* New York, 1975.

Avi-Yonah, M. *Dig This! How Archaeologists Uncover Our Past*. Minneapolis, 1993.

Beaufay, G. *Dinosaurs and Other Extinct Animals*. New York, 1987.

Briais, B. *Celts*. Tarrytown, NY, 1991.

Chenel, P. *Life and Death of Dinosaurs*. New York, 1987.

Corbishley, M. *The Celts Activity Book*. New York, 1994.

Discovery Atlas of Planets and Stars. Skokie, IL, 1993.

Duke, K. *Archaeologists Dig Square Holes*. New York, 1997.

Exploring Space: From Ancient Legends to the Telescope to Modern Space Missions. New York, 1994.

Graham, I. *Astronomy*. Chatham, NJ, 1995.

Hadingham, E. *Secrets of the Ice Age: A Reappraisal of Prehistoric Man*. New York, 1981.

Henbest, N. *The Night Sky*. Tulsa, OK, 1993.
Hoobler, D. *The Fact or Fiction Files: Lost Civilizations*. New York, 1992.

Hubble, E. *Realm of the Nebulae*. New York, 1991.

Imbrie, J. *Ice Ages: Solving the Mystery*. Cambridge, MA, 1986.

Jacobs, F. *Cosmic Countdown: What Astronomers Have Learned About the Life of the Universe*. New York, 1983.

Kerrod, Robin. *The Solar System*. Tarrytown, NY, 1993.

Let's Discover the Prehistoric World. Chatham, NJ, 1981.

Lyell, Charles. *The Neolithic Revolution*. San Diego, 1980.

Minelli, Giuseppe. *Dinosaurs and Birds*. New York, 1988.

Moeschl, Richard. *Exploring the Sky: Projects for Beginning Astronomers*. Chicago, 1992.

Moody, Richard T. *Over Sixty-five Million Years Ago: Before the Dinosaurs Died*. New York, 1992.

Nardo, Don. *Charles Darwin*. New York, 1993.

Ridpath, Ian. *Atlas of Stars and Planets*. New York, 1993.

Time-Life Books. *Space and Planets*. New York, 1991.

Illustration credits

Index

Text is indicated in roman type; illustrations are indicated in italic type.

Text is indicated in roman type; illustrations are indicated in italic type.

Text is indicated in roman type; illustrations are indicated in italic type.

Text is indicated in roman type; illustrations are indicated in italic type.